MANIFEST IT!

MANIFEST IT!

DR. CHRISTINE TOPJIAN

Christine Topjian Publishing

Contents

The Importance of Manifesting		1
Introduction		2
Dedications		4
Acknowledgements		5
1	What Is Manifesting and Why Bother?	6
2	Everyone Has Dreams	21
3	The Holy Spirit	29
4	Free Will	46
5	God Will Bring It...But We Have to Ask & Listen	54
6	God Has Already Done His Part. You Already Have It.	59
7	The Right Way and the Wrong Way	65
8	Strategic Actions	71
9	Vision Boards	76
10	Live It!	86
11	5 Keys To Manifesting Successfully	93
12	Believing In You and Jesus Working Together	97
13	The Way We Think	101
14	How To Keep In Faith While Waiting	107

15	It Manifested! Now What??	111
16	Where You Start Doesn't Matter. Just Start.	119
17	Do I Have To Already Have a Relationship with God?	123
18	Powerful Acts	128
19	Seeing And Focusing On The Fine Details	138
20	Seeing It When It Is Not Yet Physically There	148
21	The Courage To Manifest	158
22	Thoughts and Reflections	167

About the Author   175

The Importance of Manifesting

Before you read my intro. I wanted to take a moment to acknowledge and talk about the importance of manifesting! Manifesting is co-creating with God and making sure that you are bringing to reality and to the physical those wonderful dreams, and visions you have.

Who do I mean by "you"? I mean everyone. Manifesting can be done at any time and by any person. It takes work but it is worth it! Manifesting is a practice we engage in as often as possible and brings to your lived reality a new and wonderful experience that God has called you to.

How do I know this? Simple. I have lived it. I cannot (as an author) write about something I have not experienced and seen the success of for myself. Manifesting is a regular practice we need to dedicate ourselves to and it works! Also, manifesting is work! It takes focus, energy, concentration, time and much effort. It takes all of these things because visualizing one time will not be enough to cut it. You need to continue to engage in the act and it takes time each day to do it and to do it the way it needs to be done for full manifestation.

And for those wondering, manifesting is absolutely biblical. It is a practice that is rooted in the Bible and is a practice that has been gifted to us by God in order to bring His best to us and in order to bring His perfect will for us to pass.

Introduction

This book is intended to be your go-to book to explain how to achieve the lifestyle you are being guided to by God. God wants the best for us (always!) and so when we take the time to see ourselves as the best version of ourselves based on what He is guiding, we can clearly see that certain steps must be taken so we can access that "very best".

This book will draw on Biblical Scripture as evidence, will draw on infamous quotes from those who have manifested successfully and will provide you with exercises where you can learn more and begin to put the concepts mentioned into practice. Putting the concepts mentioned into regular practice is necessary for the kind of success everyone desires. Everyone desires certain things and I have never met two people who desire all of the exact same things in every area of their lives, so this book necessarily covers anything you could ever be guided to desire at any point in time of your life and within any area or domain based on God's will for you and based on what the Holy Spirit is communicating to you. How does one book do that? Simple. It's the same procedure no matter what you are called to so as long as you are doing that procedure and you are doing it consistently, regardless of what you desire, with belief, you will achieve it.

Some people picking up this book do not know God or don't know much about Him. II is never too late to begin that relationship. As an author, to show my respect, I always put a capital H when I am referring to God because He deserves it. Simply. So, for those who don't know God or His personality, I can tell you the following: He always wants the best for all His children and will always respond when you call on Him for any reason, at any time, in any way.

So whether you are a Church-goer or not, He will respond.
Whether you are one who doesn't believe in Him or does, He will respond.
Whether you feel you are a mess or you feel that you have a pretty good handle on things, He will respond.

If you need to talk to Him at 3 am or 3 pm, He will always listen, love and respond.

His responses are always loving, full of care, full of empathy and the responses of a Father who loves you and always wants the best for you, so His responses, love and guidance toward you will always come from that place of much love. God is also a respecter of persons, meaning He won't just barge into your life and take over. No. He would like to be invited, He would like to be asked, He would like you to choose (there's that free will thing again) to talk to Him and to listen to Him.

I hope this book will do all the things it sets out to do in your life and in the lives of others who also pick up this book and, or to whom you choose to gift the book to. Please also feel free to refer to my website where I have add-on teaching, notes, reminders and helpful worksheets you can use and download for free at DrChristineTopjian.com.

I also love hearing from readers (or potential readers) who would like to ask me questions about my books, resources, journals, day planners, devotionals, etc., so please feel free to use the contact form on my site and ask away!

Happy reading and happy manifesting!

Dedications

I dedicate this book to each person who desires to manifest God's will for their lives. When you do as God says and you stay in faith, trust that you will manifest all good things.

Acknowledgements

I would like to first acknowledge the Holy Spirit for not only inspiring me to write these words but also for helping me write this book at every step. Thank You.

I would also like to acknowledge the wonderful sermons and videos of Joel Osteen, whose work give me such motivation and inspiration. We all go through moments where we need another to help provide a pick-me-up and Joel's work is amazing for doing just that. Thank you

I

What Is Manifesting and Why Bother?

Manifesting is a human being's ability to co-create something that exists only in his or her mind and heart and bring it to an experiential, lived reality. In other words, to be able to see something (an event, a happening, an occurrence) in your mind and to bring the manifestation to a physical, lived reality.

Manifesting is done using a specific set of tools that God gave us and demonstrated to us back in Biblical times. We make our abilities to manifest strongest by:

1. Beginning and developing an active, loving, vibrant relationship with God.
2. Praying regularly and nurturing that relationship with God daily.
3. Accepting to receive visions from God of something He wants to bring to our reality and being open to the fact that it is a vision from God.
4. Asking about and sensing the action steps that need to be taken in the accomplishment of that vision or dream.

5. Giving thanks and gratitude.
6. Continually checking-in (daily) with the Holy Spirit.

1. Beginning and developing an active, loving, vibrant relationship with God.

This is a hugely important step and it has to be the first step. When we enter into that relationship with God, we are opening ourselves up to all the good He wants to bring into our lives. This is very important because with everything God guides us to do, there are certain actions we need to take. If we don't take those actions, we will not end up with His best for us. This necessarily therefore means that we need to develop that active and vibrant relationship with Him.

I want to tell you here that it is very possible that God will have you just focus on this for some time before He really begins to guide you. Know that He is not a God who wastes time so either way, you are using your time very wisely.

It is important (in this step) to get to know His personality very well because we need to know about the One who is leading us. Being led takes a certain amount of trust and as such, we need to make sure that we are building that trust relationship with Him.

2. Praying regularly and nurturing that relationship daily.

The most important conversation we have in our day is the one we have with God while we are in prayer. This is very important because He is our Creator, our Touchstone, our Go-to. He is the One that breathed His life into us (Genesis 2:7), He is the One who knows us, He is the One who has planned out each day of our lives for us and the blessings He always meant for us to have. This is one of the most important ways in which we build relationship with Him : by spending time with Him. It makes sense that in order to have that closeness with God where we are led by Him, we need to spend some time with Him. Even if that means 15 means here, 5 minutes there, it's still time and it still counts. It is very important because He is always talking, always willing and seeking to guide us to His best. You cannot access His best if you are not listening and paying attention to what He is saying.

We are to seek the Creator, not just what He provides.

Praying means talking directly to God about how you feel about that vision, about your thoughts about it, and about anything else you choose to communicate to Him **and** listening and waiting for His replies, His help, His guidance. Praying is meant to be a two-way conversation so this necessarily means that He will be talking to us in return about what we are praying about. This is also where you would ask what you need to do to make this vision come to life. For example, in the case above about the new career, the person would need to pray and ask what they need to do to bring that vision to come to pass. Do they need to put in their resume and their application at that particular company? What are some divine things they should say during the interview? How should they dress and present themselves at the interview? Perhaps they should visualize themselves sitting at their new desk, taking calls and getting things done.

3. Accepting to receive visions from God of something He wants to bring to our reality and being open to the fact that it is a vision from God.

God enjoys giving visions to all of us. He gives visions by allowing us to see a mental movie in our mind of something He wants to bring to pass. This means that He has determined that this reality would be very good for you and therefore, He has decided that He would like to bring it to you.

You may not be at a point in your life where you are looking for a change. You may in fact be wondering why this vision is even coming to you because you are content with things as they are. God sees 360 degrees, He knows what's coming and He can see how you will need this.

For example, God can bring you a vision of you being in and working at that new job. He can show you the letter of offer that you got the job, He can show you how happy you will be when you receive it, He can show you your first day of work. He can and does want to show you the good things He wants to bring you.

A vision can be brought to us at any time. We can be walking down the street and we see a vision. We can be lying on our couch and see a vision of something God wants to bring us for our future. We can be sitting, eating lunch and He can show us a vision. Visions can come at any time and they are powerful. But one thing in particular to note is that just because God gives you a vision, it is not a guarantee that He will bring to come to pass. In fact, a vision is His way of letting you know that this is something He wants to bring you and He is saying He desires to bring to us - but the other part of the equation is what will we do to bring that vision to life with our strategic actions.

Yes, we do need to take actions on that vision and to ask Him "What do You want me to do about this? What do You say needs to be done to make this happen?" Then, pay attention. Listen carefully, be mindful to ask about all aspects of it.

A friend of mine was happy in his marriage and was happy as a clam. When he told me one day that he had received a vision about something, he was perplexed by the vision because it had to do with a new wife by his side. He had been happily married for years and to his knowledge and understanding, he was happily married. What he didn't know was what God knew. His wife was about to leave after she had been unfaithful to him and he was going to have a very hard time with it. He was telling me that he had never imagined that he was going to have to get back into dating, back to needing a wife - he thought everything was great in his marriage but God knew better. He asked me if counseling can be done, if the marriage could be salvaged. What he wasn't factoring in is that his wife was not going to be amenable to that. She had already checked out of the marriage. I advised him to pray about it and to let God speak to his heart about his marriage - to let God show him what was really going on in his marriage - not just the flowery version he had been thinking it was. God did indeed show him when He began to unveil the lies, the deception and the affairs she had had along the way.

God sees all and God knows all, and when He gives a vision, we need to pay attention. In the particular case of my friend, he needed to allow God to open his eyes and to show him what he wasn't seeing and what he didn't want to see.

> **They are things He is saying He desires to bring to us - the other part of the equation is what will we do to bring that vision to life with our strategic actions.**

4. Asking about and sensing the action steps that need to be taken in the accomplishment of that vision.

Everything in life requires action steps that need to be done. Everything. There are no exceptions to that and while we may have a sense of what needs to be done, we need to check-in and ask God for what He says needs to be done.

This is the part of prayer where we need to ask what needs to be done and we need to ask God to guide our steps. When you do this, be prepared to sense things and to write down feelings and senses that you are getting. Many people get into the practice of sitting in prayer, asking for what needs to be done and writing down what they get: senses, action steps, etc., and that's a great practice to get into.

5. Giving Thanks and Gratitude.

God has already given us much, we owe it to Him to say thank You (the capital Y is meant to denote respect). Everything that we have in our lives is a direct result of what God has brought to us, from the air in our lungs, to the organs in our body, to our ability to breathe in deeply, to our ability to reason things out and to use our minds for good and for advancement, and the list goes on. Giving thanks daily would not be too much to ask. Giving thanks regularly in advance of receiving the things you want and ask for is a great practice to get into.

Having a gratitude journal or a dedicated space to write out your thanks to Him and the blessings He has already brought you is a powerful and beautiful tool. Reminding ourselves regularly that we already have some wonderful blessings is a very helpful way of reminding ourselves and encouraging ourselves that we already have much because He has already brought much. If He has already provided those things, why do we think He won't provide other things He has put on our hearts?

6. Continually checking-in (daily) with the Holy Spirit to make sure that we are doing things as God wants them to be done, in the ways that He wants them done and in the time frame in which He wants them done. This is really important as well because things change, circumstances change and we need to keep checking-in with God to see what's next, what He wants us to do, and much more.

Examples of Things God Can Put On Your Heart

God always wants the best for us. This is true to His nature of loving all of His children. You do not need to be in "this" particular career or come from "this" particular family in order for Him to want to bless you. He loves all His children (talk about inclusive!) and He has had good things planned for every single one of us from the beginning of time and from the beginning of our creation.

As such, He will find ways to put on your heart and to communicate His will for you. He will find ways of letting you know blessings He wishes to bring to you. Each morning when we wake up, it is important to remind ourselves of this because when we lose sight of this, depression, anxiety and many more such things can begin to creep up in our lives. We have to regularly remind ourselves that He wills the best things for us and that He will find ways to communicate those desires to us. Our part is to listen, accept and take the steps that are needed to receive.

There are so many examples of things that God can put on our hearts to enrich our lives and to make things better. The list of what He can do and can provide in our lives is literally endless because God owns it all, can do literally anything and is never limited to the natural realm. He did bring water out of a rock in the Bible and He can and still does perform such awesome miracles today too!

We can also literally bring about anything into our lives. Read that statement again because that's how important it is to realize that. When we close our eyes and imagine ourselves having received everything, we are exercising a gift that He has given us. It is the gift of manifesting! Manifesting literally means to make something we desire appear into our lives, in the physical, very real sense.

I will provide an example: upon receiving the words for my first book by the Lord, I knew that I wanted to have it traditionally published. This was important to me and I felt that it was something God had put on my heart. I closed my eyes (not just once but many times) and I imagined it, over and over again. I saw in my mind's eye the manifestation of this dream. I saw everything from the actual contract in my email inbox to the book appearing both online and in bookstores. I looked carefully at the fine details of my new contract and the favorable terms, even though I was a first-timer. I saw all the little details and even looked carefully at the thickness of the pages of the book. It was all extraordinary and I felt every happy feeling of this accomplishment. I had to wait a little while but I did indeed get my first publishing contract. It was for my first book, Jesus Loves You. I am as happy today as I was back then at having published this book.

We can literally imagine anything as coming to fruition in our lives. Literally anything. Of course, it is important that we ask God if that thing is in fact His will for us because things that are contrary to the nature of God are not desires brought to you from Him. Some of those things can include: murder, rape, lying and cheating, deceiving others, and more that are totally contrary to the personality of God.

It's Work!

One of the things that I realized for myself when I began visualizing through meditation and asking the Holy Spirit for His help and guidance on this is that it takes time and it is work! Manifesting takes work, tremendous focus, dedication and strategic action. If you are not doing it the way it is supposed to be done, the chances are quite unlikely that you are going to experience the success of this. If you do not take the inspired and strategic actions required, you are not fulfilling all the requirements. For example, if you know that you want to be a published author and you do spend time visualizing that, you also have to take the inspired and strategic actions required. You have to spend the time writing your book, editing, perfecting all of it, working on the fine details of how to properly submit your manuscript, and more. It takes time, work and dedication but they are the actions that will be required. Many people say that they haven't received what they were praying and visualizing for. When I ask what actions they took to these ends, they usually admit that they didn't fulfill the other requirement: working on it.

This is a great point in the book where I would like to show and explain some things you can do to cause things to manifest.

- If God has put the desire on your heart to enroll in a certain University, you can begin to cause the manifestation of that by imagining that you receive the letter admitting you to the school and how happy you will feel when you have that admissions letter in your hands, even as far as seeing and feeling the thickness of the paper which you imagine holding in your hands. You can see yourself sending the email accepting the offer of admission, you can see yourself enrolling for your first classes and seeing yourself in the lecture hall of your first classes.
- If God has put the desire on your heart to get a job at a certain company, you can begin to see yourself sitting at your desk at company headquarters, booting up your email and seeing yourself doing the very work you would like to be doing, being a team member in the department in which you would like to be in. See yourself talking to and collaborating with whom you imagine your boss would be and how he or she would be super impressed with the ideas you are bringing forward.
- If God has put the desire on your heart to be a parent, see yourself taking the pregnancy test and it revealing a positive "pregnant" result. See yourself celebrating this with your spouse and see yourself going shopping for baby furniture. Do all the things

that you would like to do, as though you are already pregnant and feel the feelings of great joy that you know you would be feeling if it were already in your reality.
- If God has put the desire on your heart to start a business, you can spend time each day seeing yourself at the helm of your company, wearing many hats (as entrepreneurs tend to do) and working hard at establishing your client base and your company website. It would be wise to see the successes of acquiring new paying clients, actually being paid, delivering great work that wows your clients, even seeing the happy and impressed looks on the faces of your clients as you put forward the great work you have prepared.
- If God has put the desire on your heart to travel around the world, getting paid to do this, begin to see yourself on the planes, traveling from wherever you are to wherever you want to go, your luggage in hand and see yourself at all the destinations you wish to go to. See your bank account balance increasing with each trip you take and feel the happiness that will inevitably result when you see the success of each part of what you are doing.
- If God has put the desire on your heart to be a great performer, see yourself getting the roles you desire, the employment contract in your inbox and see (down to the finest details) what favourable contractual terms you are being offered. See yourself on the set or on the stage, actually performing, putting your all into it and how captivated you imagine the audience to be, amazed at your performance and loving every moment. At the end, imagine the highest of tv or movie ratings and revenue, or for the stage, imagine your standing ovation night after night.
- If you have a desire to be a great Principal, see yourself receiving the offer from the organization, presenting you with favorable contractual terms and your start date. See your staff responding favorably to you and see yourself managing the school and all the pieces that would be involved with that with great ease and success.

It is very important to dedicating yourself to seeing the minute and finite aspects of each thing you desire. The Lord and the world will respond favorably. You will be able to attain the things you desire if you remain steadfast in your practice and you confidently take the inspired and strategic actions that will be required.

Why You Want It

If your desire is in-line with God's personality of love and provision, your desire of it is because God has put that desire on your heart. He is signaling to you that you already have that thing in the Spirit realm. It is already yours with your name on it. All you have to do is start acting like you have it, start thinking like you have it, and keep taking the strategic actions needed for its attainment.

In other words, God foresaw all that we would need. He foresaw and planned for it all and He specifically provided for all that we would need. As such, He also provided a means in which we can help ourselves achieve it. He would not give us a desire that He cannot or will not bring to fulfill. That is not in His personality. He is the One who has put the dream on your heart, to excel and to set a new standard for you, for your family and for your community. You are never alone in what you are trying to do. He created you and He has prepared everything you need to accomplish those dreams, to do all that He has called you to do. This necessarily implies that if he has called you to be a great actor, you already have the skills to be so. If He has called you to a great surgeon, He has already given you the skills to be so. The list is literally endless.

Does that mean we don't need schooling or training ever again? Of course not. Schooling and training are meant to enhance and to bring to light and to our conscious the skills that we already have and the talents that He has already put in us. Plus, schooling and training are excellent opportunities to push ourselves and our skill sets far beyond.

I remember when I was applying to the Christian Leadership University for my Doctorate program, I already knew that I was good at two-way journaling. I already knew that because I had been doing it for well over two years already at that point. A huge part of the program was engaging in two-way journaling and so being in the program was my opportunity to further enhance and develop those skills, to further gain insight into this great skill and to further my relationship with God, more than it already was.

When a friend of mine was in the process of writing her first book, she had asked me if I could help her probe the Holy Spirit and try to find out more about what God wanted to say to people through her and her book. She shared with me that she had covered the topics that she thought she was being led to cover but felt something was missing. Together, we probed the Holy Spirit to see if something else would need to be written and sure enough, plenty more direction came through, with plenty more topics that were offshoots from the main, central topic. Her manuscript went from being 100 pages to over 350, full of the additional details the Holy Spirit was guiding her into considering and covering in the book.

Here is an example of this probing. I know how important examples are when we are trying to learn. This is an actual conversation of mine with the Holy Spirit.

Me: Thank You for guiding me with the words I have included thus far in the book, Holy Spirit. What else do You want me to convey in this book?

H.S.: Very important to talk about the topics and the methods for visualizing and manifesting. These are extremely important topics that people from all walks of life and people with dreams and desires as varied and as important as earth itself need to know about. Every provision has been provided to all people, even though where it may seem that they don't have the necessary. If a person does not have something or thinks they do not have something that is needed, they are to ask Me (in their mind or with words, it doesn't matter) and I will speak to their hearts about it. I, the Lord, always provide. Always and in every way. Everything is mine to give and so when My faithful children follow (and faithful means that they do things in tandem with Me), I will provide more than enough. Always.

Me: I see. Ok. What else do You want me to convey to people? Any other teachings?

H.S.: People do not ask and then they complain that I did not provide. Everything is provided and where they don't see it provided, they have to ask and it will either be given or I will highlight and point out how they already have it. All My children ever have to do is ask and believe that they are receiving. They have to ask and believe in the receipt. Spending time alone and in quiet with Me will teach them of My goodness, My provision, My heart for them and how I can and have provided for them in every situation. If you have not, it is because they have not asked or they have not yet taken the steps I have led them to take.

Me: How do You want people to ask if they may not believe in You?

H.S.: Test Me. Ask and test Me. Many in this world do not believe Me or don't believe in Me. Test Me I tell you and you will see what I will do. Those who ask will always be provided with the means. A person can come from the poorest parts of the world but because they have asked and they have faith, I will always provide or I have already provided.

Me: Thank You, Holy Spirit.

H.S.: Keep asking. Ask Me more things.

Me: Ok. Since this is a book on manifesting, what do You say are the most important parts to manifesting?

H.S.: Believe that you already have it because you do. You have it in the Spirit and the world just takes some time to bring it down to your lived reality. In your mind (eyes open or closed doesn't matter), see yourself (the microscopic details) of that reality and see how you have accomplished it. If you want to see it brought down to earth more quickly, say so. Say "Holy Spirit, bring this thing or these things to me in record quick time. Shorten the waiting time to 0." See what happens. I always provide because it is all Mine to provide. Schools don't teach this anymore and so people lack the practice in doing this. It is such an important prayer (yes, that was a prayer) and this is a vital part of the process. Ask and ye shall receive. Knock and the door will be opened. Seek and it shall be given to you.

Me: Thank You, Holy Spirit.

H.S.: Ask Me at least one more question before closing this section. I desire for people to see that they need to keep asking, to keep probing for more detail and for more information. If you don't have it yet, it's because you need to ask Me to bring it right away. There is nothing wrong with being respectfully forceful about it.

Me: Ok. When people have asked and they haven't yet received, what are some ways that they can wait in the right way(s)?

H.S.: Excellent question. Keep asking, keep praying, keep visualizing and keep asking for more detail about it. For many, they do not keep asking (they ask once and that's it) and for others, they lack asking for details. The details are very important because if I am guiding someone to take a particular step, to do this particular thing, they may not see why that action step is important in the overall picture, but that's where trust comes in. Trust that I am properly guiding them, showing them the way and opening what needs to be opened in the right way and at the right time.

Me: And people can freely ask You for wisdom and clarity in understanding that too, right?

H.S.: They are always invited to and I will always respond. I can be in a million places at once and I can speak to a billion hearts and minds at once. That is part of My power and I created each person so that they can easily hear from Me. Imagine My sadness when I see that people don't want to hear from Me, don't want My help or want to do things on their own. They are unnecessarily making life a million times harder for themselves. Neither man nor woman was ever meant to do everything on his or her own. I love all My children and wish to guide all of them to the greatest levels of abundance and prosperity. True.

Me: Thank You, Holy Spirit. I pray that these words really sink into peoples minds and peoples hearts and that they open themselves up to a greater relationship with You and for those who don't know You, that they open themselves up to a relationship with You. In Jesus' name. Amen

2

Everyone Has Dreams

Everyone Has Dreams

Fact: We all have dreams. We all have many things we wish to accomplish in our lives and that's awesome. Dreams give our lives more meaning, they fuel our day and they are the gas for fuel of every one of our actions.

> **Faith is the currency of Heaven and it is faith, inspired God-given actions and thanksgiving together that move God to do great things on our behalf.**

God didn't just plant those dreams in our hearts so that they can remain things we long for. He planned for those desires He knew we would have and prepared the way for you to achieve and attain those things. He also knew that by making you a co-creator with Him, that He would be activating the faith muscles inside of you because creating depends on our faith in Him. Faith is the currency of Heaven and it is faith, inspired God-given actions and thanksgiving together that move God to do great things on our behalf. As such, we need to tap into this wonderful opportunity and we are invited to make sure that we are co-creating with Him. How do we do this? **Through prayer and visualization.**

Prayer

Prayer means a two-way conversation with God. In prayer, we present our requests to Him and ask Him to talk to us about them. Through the advent of prayer, God responds to us by giving us sensations, feelings, words of wisdom and guides us. Even if you don't have that close relationship with God just yet, prayer is still an excellent idea just to unload, to get things off your chest, to talk to God and to help you start feeling better because you are getting it out.

Intercessory prayer: This is an important add-on to this section about prayer. Intercessory prayer is when we pray on someone else's behalf. For example, if someone does not feel able to pray or they can't at that moment, another person can intercede on their behalf and can ask the Lord for things on their behalf. You can literally intercede about anything that is likely to be in God's will and you can do this for anyone. For example, it would not be in God's will for you to kill someone for someone else, so even if you pray this in intercessory prayer, this prayer will not be answered and the action completed. For example, when people ask others to pray for a loved one who is going through difficulty of some kind, this is an excellent example of intercessory prayer because showing others love and kindness is very important and is definitely something God calls us to do. An unlimited number of people can engage in intercessory prayer.

Visualization

Through visualization, we are provided with images and "mini-movies" if you will, that give us an idea of what God wants to bring to us. We can see these mini movies just as we would a regular movie, except this would be in the eyes of our mind and in the eyes of our heart. **You would need to use the power and muscles of your imagination to be able to see and visualize these things clearly and decisively, making room for them in your mind and in your heart.** You may notice that the more you undertake this practice, the more "used to" you begin becoming to this new reality, even if this is not a practice you have previously ever undertaken. You can begin to experience this new reality and you may (as some have previously reported doing) even take a step of feeling mentally taken aback by what you are seeing because this vision is so new to you.

When most people receive vision, it usually takes some time for people to fully process that vision. Why? Well because it is a new, lived reality. As humans, we tend to be creatures of habit and routine, so when we are presented with a new image and a new reality, it can definitely take some time for that to sink in. It is a phenomenal process and one that we may very well need to rely on God to help us with. And there is nothing wrong with relying on Him to help us with it. I recall the first time I received a vision about something, it was not something I wanted to happen. In fact, it had to do with a matter of the heart so I actually didn't want the vision to come true. But I knew that it was God's will for that to happen and so I had to accept it and I did do my part in helping to ensure that it was done and in the way that it needed to be.

Hurts the Flesh

There will be times where what God wants you to do will, frankly, suck. It will hurt your flesh and you won't want to do it. I speak from experience because as in the example above, I didn't want to do what the Lord had called me to do and it really took everything in me (strength-wise) to be obedient and to do it. The point: sometimes the actions will hurt but having faith and respect in God means that we have to find and pray for the strength to do it even when it does hurt.

If you are being called to do something like that, pray for the strength to do it. Praying for the strength to do something is very important because oftentimes, without that prayer answered, we won't actually be able to do what needs to be done. Pray for the strength and sometimes, it helps to just sit in a moment of silence and let yourself be washed with God's grace and His Spirit of strength.

The Science of It

> The fact is: In the human mind, there is little difference between experiencing the desired reality in your mind and experiencing the desired reality in concrete reality so your brain cannot tell the difference between this perceived reality and reality.

Manifesting is one of the most important acts a human being can take on, closely resembling prayer in importance and in impact. In fact, one might even argue that the process to achieve manifestation, which is visualizing, is akin to prayer. You see, God can read and see our very hearts and our very souls. When we visualize, just like when we pray, God can see our true desires, our true intentions and our true motivations. He sees all and knows us better than we know ourselves. He created us with the ability to pray, meditate and visualize, not to mention to have a sound mind and to reason things out. This therefore means that visualizing is the process of creating in your mind (using your imagination and the help of the Holy Spirit) the lived reality of the very things you desire for yourself, which God has put on your heart. I will then take it a step further and say that visualizing is one of the most important things we do in our day, because it is our communication with God that "this" (that He has put on our heart) is so important to me that I am dedicating time each day to the practice of visualizing it. It is saying that I believe this is the way You are guiding me to achieve "that thing" and so I will dedicate my time to doing it and to investing in Your will for it.

It doesn't matter if your ideal is any of the following or a combination of any of the following (list is below), the point is: it's important enough to you and you believe God is leading you to that thing so this is your response to say "I'm on board, Lord, and I'm willing to show You just how much I desire to co-create that with You. I am showing You through the process of my daily actions just how much I am on board with You and just how much I am dedicating myself to the acquisition of this."

List of things a person could possibly desire (this is not an exhaustive list, of course):

- Getting into a certain school
- Being the recipient of a full scholarship to be in the program you have gotten into
- Being popular and well-liked by people
- Having and being in possession of good health
- Having and being in possession of good wealth
- Having a healthy, close-knit family
- Meeting and marrying your God-given soulmate
- Having happy and healthy children (your biological own or adopted ones)

- Having a well-paying, satisfying career
- Having and realizing the ability to be promoted in one's career or for a spouse or partner for their career
- Having a successful start-up business and being your own boss
- Feeling happy inside each day
- Having your family and friends feeling happy inside each day
- Having a certain mode of transportation
- Being a great thinker
- Being able to love ourselves
- Actually engaging in the process of loving ourselves
- Being a great speaker/orator
- No matter the industry you find yourself in or you would like to be in, finding success with that
- Being closer to God, Jesus and the Holy Spirit
- Protection from all kinds of negative and bad things
- Being able to afford, and to make healthy foods that are nourishing for the mind, body and soul
- Being organized
- Being tidy
- Having a healthy and happy pet
- Being able to breath in deeply and go for a walk outside
- Having harmonious relationships
- Clarity of mind and of vision
- Being able to get a good night's sleep

There are millions more items I could have added to the list but I would like to use this opportunity to give you a chance to add to this list with things that you believe God has put on your heart. As you can see, I have included blessings for yourself, for those around you, for people from all walks of life, for all ages and all interests and you can do the same when it comes to your list: include things for yourself and for others. The bottom line is:

> Everyone wants things. Everyone desires things.

Take a moment now and jot down the items for your list.

_____
_____
_____
_____
_____
_____
_____
_____
_____
_____
_____
_____
_____
_____
_____
_____
_____
_____
_____
_____
_____

Consistency

The question then becomes: are you willing to do (consistently) what God has instructed you to do to acquire that thing? The realization of your goal or dream may not happen overnight and so we need to be consistent at the steps needed in order to achieve or ascertain something. This consistency when you have not yet seen the realization of your dream or goal is what we refer to as consistent and persistent work. It can be challenging because it is continuing to work at something when you have not yet seen the manifestation of it just yet. But we have to keep "continuing on" in order to see that success in our minds and the manifestation in real life.

People who have a walk with God and who have already reached (or are reaching) the level of success that they desired, have done exactly what the Lord has guided them to do to acquire that thing or those things, and consistently so. Today, they are reaping the benefits of what they sowed.

If you haven't already done so, are you willing to do all that He is guiding you to do through the promptings of the Holy Spirit?

Here is a little prayer you can pray to have the stamina to keep going if you have not yet seen the reality of your dream but you are doing all that was required.

Lord, thank You for putting the dream on my heart to do _____. I feel (or believe) that I have done and am doing all that You have guided me to do. If there is something that I have not done and that still requires to be done, please let me know. I pray for Your strength and Your help as I wait for the realization and the manifestation of what You have called me to do. In Jesus' name. Amen

3

The Holy Spirit

The Holy Spirit is our Helper, our Counselor, our Friend, our Mentor, our Truth-Teller and dwells on the inside of us. As such, we cannot "lose the Holy Spirit" in the sense that as long as we are checking-in and continuing to engage Him, we will always have Him there. Whether it's 2 am or 2 pm, He is there to help us, to guide us, to be a beacon of light and of hope and to help us by giving us the detailed steps that are required for the attainment of that goal, not to mention peace, comfort, truth and much more.

God never asked or asks us to figure out the steps to success, life, happiness, abundance and goodness on our own. God never said that He was tasking us with doing that. Instead, He guides us to the Holy Spirit who is our Helper and we are supposed to rely on His guidance and His specific instructions to help us.

"This Way or That Way?" - the Holy Spirit Will Guide You.

The Holy Spirit is the very Spirit of God and He is there to help us, to guide us, and to provide for us. Because He is the Spirit of God, He can see things at 360 degrees (which we cannot) and as such, we would be wise to go to Him and ask for the help that we need. He will provide us with insights that we could not have known on our own and viewpoints that we could not have seen coming.

No matter what the question is, and in what context, ask Him. Each step you take and each decision you make is an important (even vital) piece of the puzzle and it is so important that you realize that He is guiding you to His best, not a regular human's best.

I encourage you to read the testimonials of people who have blindly followed the Holy Spirit (even when it didn't make sense at the time) and they have benefited significantly because of it. The 700 Club is one of my absolutely favorite go-tos for that.

The Holy Spirit….Our Motivator

One of the most important things that is needed today is motivation. People need much motivation to help them, to keep them on-task and to keep them on "keeping on". As such, we need to ask the Holy Spirit is there to help us with that. All we have to do is access Him and ask Him. It's free and always available (sounds like a pretty good deal to me)!

I know that for myself, when I am feeling a bit low and I need that pick-me-up or I am feeling a bit discouraged, I need to go to the Holy Spirit for His help and His guidance. I need to pray for strength and wisdom and for Him to show me how what I am doing is the right thing. I also need to know that for the people to whom I minister, this is also the case and I need to ask the Holy Spirit that I am ministering to them in the right ways, saying the right things and using strategies that will work for that specific person and for that specific context.

Fact: We all go through difficulties in life and we can all get down. But God has never asked us to figure it all out for ourselves. No, He specifically says that it is very important for us to go to Him and to get the help of the Holy Spirit in accomplishing anything, including help in manifesting something.

Yes, It Is a Gift

Being able to manifest is a gift. It takes time, dedication, patience, faith, belief, action and more and manifesting is your reward for having done those things. All of the qualities mentioned in the previous sentence are all equally important to the process of manifesting. I will go into each of these parts in more depth so that you fully understand the full picture.

Time: Manifesting does take time and so you need to be visualizing a little each day (at least 15 mins.) and then, giving things time for the reality to be created and for it all to come together and to come to you. Please also factor in the time that it will take to overcome the inevitable challenges that will come.

Dedication: Because manifesting doesn't usually happen overnight, we do need to take time to dedicate to this practice and to repeatedly "see" this new reality in our minds and in our hearts. Dedication necessarily implies that just because you are not seeing it today, tomorrow or next week, it doesn't mean you should stop visualizing it or stop working on it.

Patience: Patience implies that even when you don't see it appearing right away but that you are following all the steps required, that you will be patient because you will be seeing it manifest itself. You do need to give it some time.

Faith: Faith is a must in this equation because we are using the eyes of our hearts and minds to believe that God is bringing this thing to us and that even though we may not see things coming together to provide the fruit in front of us just yet, that we know it is on its way to us. God has done His part and provided the means, we just need to stick with it.

Belief in yourself: Part of the equation is that you need to believe in your own abilities to visualize and to manifest. We are all capable of doing this but if you are not believing in your own abilities to co-create with God, half the battle is already lost.

Belief in God: Ultimately, it is God who is going to bring the manifestation of this blessing to you. It was His will for you to have it which is why He put the desire for it on your heart. As such, believe in Him and in His goodness that He will be bringing this to you.

Action: You must take strategic actions that are Spirit-led and Spirit-inspired. In life, things don't tend to just drop into our laps. We generally need to take strategic actions to see something come to pass.

Not listening to naysayers: Unfortunately, not everyone is going to be your cheerleader. There will always be people who are not "for you" and don't want to see the best come to you. Never mind those people. You swim your best proverbial race and you do your best, despite what they say. If you have negative people actively in your face, remind them that they don't need to be there and shut that negativity out. You have your race to run. Not everyone is meant to be your cheerleader. Scripturally, I think we can all agree that Jesus did not have everyone in His corner as His cheerleader, but He managed to persevere despite.

So Manifesting Means....

So, when a person manifests, they are actually causing something (a dream, an idea, a hope, a picture) that exists in their mind to become a lived reality in the physical sense.

* When a person who is sick with cancer begins seeing themselves as healthy, healed and whole, they are beginning to cause that reality to take shape. They are beginning to create health & happiness for themselves in the form of that reality.

* When a person who has no money begins to see themselves as wealthy and prosperous, they are beginning to cause that reality to take shape. They are beginning to create that wealth for themselves.

* When a person who has no children but desires to have children, they are beginning to cause that reality to take shape. They are beginning to create that wealth for themselves.

* When a person desires to own their own business but has little to no resources to begin but they begin to see themselves as the owner of the business, they are beginning to cause that reality to take shape. They are beginning to create that wealth for themselves.

We can begin from anywhere and can cause the new reality to manifest but that's the key: to start. Start seeing it, start praying for it, start visualizing it.

> Christian manifesting is when you dedicate yourself to bringing and seeing what Jesus wants for your life to come to pass by using the process of visualization and by having faith in what Jesus can do and can bring. Keeping our eyes on Jesus while doing this is vital.

Can Anyone Manifest?

Yes, anyone can manifest and because God has called each and every one of us to do great things, we all need to get into the habit of doing the little daily and important actions needed to get there. Christ-centered manifesting is when you dedicate yourself to bringing and seeing what God wants for your life to come to pass by using the process of visualization and by having faith in not only what God can do and can bring but what He will. Visualizing means simply seeing in your mind's eye and in your heart's eyes a visual depiction of that reality and hoping to bring it to earth. For example, if a person knows that it's God's will for them to be a doctor, while they are taking all the physical actions needed to get into and to succeed in medical school (such as succeeding in their med school classes, passing the exams, getting the grades and succeeding in their residency), they should also be taking the time to see the visuals of that success in their mind's eye and in the eyes of their heart.

Doing so is a practice that requires dedication, effort, time, and faith. Seeing it one time and then expecting it to appear is simply not sound reality. Instead, we need to see it, over and over again, again and again and keep the sustained image in the back of our minds as we go through our day, remembering to thank God in advance of its manifestation. "Thank You, God that You are bringing this to me and to my lived reality" is a great thing to say through the course of your day.

Of course, we also have to take the necessary actions required to achieve the manifestation of the reality. Going back to my previous example of being a doctor, if you don't actually go to med school and work hard at your school work, no amount of visualization will help you manifest the success you desire without the necessary actions.

"Christine, does it work?"

Yes, it does. How do I know it works? Because I have used it many times and have seen many awesome things come to pass with many others I am also still waiting for. For example, as I was visualizing many things I wished to have come to pass, one by one, I did experience the manifestation and it's a pretty great feeling. Does it work with one try? Likely not in one single try (it never has worked for me after just one time of visualizing or after one time of concentrated visualizing) so I have learned that this needs to be something you sustain on a few occasions.

All of the following are things I have watched manifest because I took the time to dedicate to visualizing and to being led to visuals by God:

- People getting better from sickness
- Unfavorable business practices ceasing and me being the benefit of it ceasing
- Money coming into my life
- Health being restored
- Solutions to problems that I couldn't have make happen on my own
- A new car having been given to me
- The right man coming into my life
- The right man telling me he wants to be with me
- Wonderful friendships coming to me and staying for a lifetime (so far, as of this writing)
- My first (and then subsequent) publishing contract
- My first career
- My Doctorate degree (just finding the right program and getting into the program was a feat all on its own)
- The health and wellness of my nephew and his mama, especially when she was about to give birth

- My close family members experiencing renewed health despite huge health setbacks

What It Looks Like

When we dedicate time each day to visualizing, we will see the manifestation of what we have visualized. It may not look like what you envisioned, but it will manifest. We have to be smart enough to recognize it despite it not looking the way we think it should.

> **It may not look like what you envisioned, but it will manifest with some time. We just have to be smart enough to recognize it despite it not looking the way we think it should.**

I say the statement just above because I have missed out on one or more of my blessings when they did manifest themselves because it didn't look the way I thought it would or should.

A lady I was ministering to had the same experience. She mentioned that she wanted to get into law school and that she had picked her favorite schools to apply to. I reminded her that it's great to have your preferences but if that (or those) are not the doors that God opens but He opens the door to a different law school, that there is nothing wrong with that and that she should be happy, satisfied and grateful with the school she gets into. People can sometimes have a romanticized view of what something is supposed to look like and if it doesn't turn out exactly as they think it should or would, they can sometimes not recognize the blessing and they can turn away from it. Luckily, in the case of this lady, she did listen to the advice and she did attend the law school she got into, which was not one of her top choices but nevertheless, she got in and realized how very blessed she was to have gotten in because it was the door God chose to open for her.

We have to also remember that when we take on a romanticized view of something, that view may not exactly be steeped in reality. In other words, we can think that the spouse of our dreams, the business of our dreams, the ideal job or the ideal situation is supposed to look like the exact image in our minds and that can cause us to miss out on something that looks different but is still very meaningful.

I caution you at this point in the book to pray to the Holy Spirit to see if the manifestation is what He intended to bring you and if it is, do not turn it down. Even if it looks different from what you thought, it is still a blessing that has manifested and so....grab it and say thanks!

The Sky Is the Limit

I am always surprised when people say that it is not ok or Godly to want many things. I ask the question: "Where did you get that idea from?" God calls us to be humble in Spirit (to be kind and generous in Spirit) but He has never said that we cannot want many things and that we should not work and visualize for many things.

Everything from the domain of careers, relationships, money and finance, the sky is the limit. And Biblically, God provides. He never asks us to want little on purpose.

I mention this because many people ask: is it ok to want lots of things? The answer is yes, of course. We have been built to want and to desire and there is nothing wrong or bad or reason to feel ashamed about that. We just need to be sure that it's a desire God has put on our hearts (and in line with His personality....refer back to my example of causing harm to another and how that cannot be God's will) and how we go about it is very important.

Many people make it harder on themselves than it needs to be, unnecessarily so. In other words, they strive, they work so very hard and they try to make it happen in their own strength (as Abraham did in the Bible) and it doesn't need to be that way. God is our Partner in making these things happen for us; He is the One who will open the right doors in the right times.

As part of my Doctorate studies, we looked in-depth at how the Bible and God's own Word supports this and we explored this thoroughly. Here are some Bible passages to help support this and each passage will be explained thoroughly. This was an important element that I wanted to include in this book for the simple reason that when I was starting on my journey of learning to visualize and to manifest, I was a bit confused on how I was supposed to pray over the dreams and goals that I felt were in me and I had to understand how (in God's way) I was supposed to access these.

Here are some examples in Scripture of how visualizing and manifesting was used.

Colossians 3:2: Set your mind on the things above, not on the things that are on earth.

Habakkuk 2:2-3: Then the Lord answered me and said,
"Record the vision
And inscribe it on tablets,
That the one who reads it may run.
For the vision is yet for the appointed time;
It hastens toward the goal and it will not fail.
Though it tarries, wait for it;
For it will certainly come, it will not delay."

Hebrews 11:27: By faith he left Egypt, not fearing the wrath of the king; for he endured, as seeing Him who is unseen.

John 1:51: And He said to him, "Truly, truly, I say to you, you will see the heavens opened and the angels of God ascending and descending on the Son of Man."

Matthew 4:8: Again, the devil took Him to a very high mountain and showed Him all the kingdoms of the world and their glory.

Genesis 15:1: After these things the word of the Lord came to Abram in a vision, saying,
"Do not fear, Abram,
I am a shield to you;
Your reward shall be very great."

Romans 4:20 - 21: Yet, with respect to the promise of God, he did not waver in unbelief but grew strong in faith, giving glory to God, and being fully assured that what God had promised, He was able also to perform.

The following excerpts were pulled from the Conversations with God Ministry of Dr. Mark Virkler, showing how many times visualizing and manifesting are mentioned in the Bible. I have found these to be tremendously helpful in my own understanding of the concepts and practices of visualizing and manifesting:

1. God gave Abraham a vision of the stars of the sky and told him he would have that many children (Gen. 15:5), and that produced faith in Abraham's heart (Gen. 15:6). So here we have an example of godly imagery which produced faith in the man who is called "the Father of Faith" (Rom. 4:11). That is a powerful concept. That

would indicate that if I wanted faith in my heart which moves mountains, then I would need the same ingredients which God gave to Abraham. These are:

- A spoken promise (Gen. 12:1,2)
- A divine picture (Gen. 15:1,5,6)

Then as I hold this promise and picture in my heart, meditate on it and ponder it, God produces a miracle in the fullness of time. For Abraham, a child was born 25 years later.

2. God has created us with eyes in our hearts with which we can see, picture and visualize.

3. God wants to fill these eyes with His dreams, visions and images (Acts 2:17).

4. Jesus lived in pictures continuously (Jn. 5:19,20,30).

5. Jesus filled the eyes of His listeners by constantly teaching with parables (Matt. 13:34).

6. We are commanded to meditate on the Word, which involves prayerfully rolling it around in our hearts and minds. Since the Bible is full of picture stories, we will by necessity be picturing as we meditate upon Scripture (Josh. 1:8). The Hebrew word "meditate" in Joshua 1:8 includes in its definition, "to imagine."

7. When we reason together with God, He uses imagery (Isa. 1:18 "sins as scarlet... white as snow").

8. A picture is worth 1000 words, so when I see something, it has the power to change me much more greatly than when I simply think a thought. That is why God says we are transformed (changed) "while we look" (2 Cor. 3:17,18; 4:16-18). When I see myself clothed with Christ's robe of righteousness (Gal. 3:27), it appears to influence me more greatly than when I simply recall the Scripture verse that "I am the righteousness of God in Christ Jesus" (Phil. 3:9).

9. God counsels us at night through our dreams (Ps. 16:7).

10. Even the Lord's supper utilizes imagery. As Jesus broke the bread,

He said, "This is My body" and as they drank the wine, He said, "This is My blood" (Matt. 26:26-28). I see this imagery as I partake of the Lord's supper, and by doing so, it impacts me greatly every time I do it.

11. The Bible is absolutely full of dreams, visions, pictures, images, and parables from cover to cover, so obviously God is big on imagery.

12. When David prayed, he used imagery (Ps. 23).

13. When David worshiped, he used imagery (Ps. 36:5,6).

14. When David walked, he pictured the Lord at His right hand (Acts 2:25; Ps. 16:8). When we "abide in Christ" (Jn. 15:4), we can use the same technique.

15. In the Tabernacle in the wilderness, God established much imagery that was an integral part of approaching Him (Ex. 25:8-22).

16. In the New Testament, we are told that Jesus is the Image of the invisible God, and we are to "fix our eyes upon Him" (Heb. 12:1,2). David was clearly visualizing the Lord at his right hand (Ps. 16:8; Acts 2:25). So in both Old and New Testaments, God has ordained imagery as part of our approach to Him.

We see in each of these passages how God has used the tools of visualization and images, mentioning how important they are as concepts, as illustrations and how they show how visualization is a God-given tool that allows us to be made aware of the will of God and to bring His will to fruition. We also know that Biblically, those who were waiting to receive the blessing had to wait significant amounts of time before the blessing happened. They had to wait years for the promise to come to manifest and in that time, they had to lean into faith in God's character that He can and He would do this for them to keep their motivation up such as. Sometimes, we can see the humanity of the people in the Bible: people who felt unsure of themselves, people who got tired and frustrated of waiting, people who fell into unbelief, so they took the matter into their own hands, people who stood there in shock and amazement while they watched God do what He did, and many more. The people for whom God did these things were ordinary, normal and regular people like you and I, and it took them a tremendous amount of faith to wait on His promises. Just like it may be taking you longer than you would like it to.

Using Vivid Visual & Literary Imagery

In one of the passages above, we are presented with such a literary parallel of "sins as scarlet". A detailed description like that goes a long way to helping us see conceptually how red the thing that is being described was and it goes a long way to qualifying what God wants us to know about something. He wants us to see just how red the item is that He is talking about. He is not saying it is a bit red or it is an orangy-red. No, He means scarlet red and if you think about it, without that parallel, we can imagine sins to be red but there are so many variations of the shades of red, of how much red, was it a translucent red. Without the literary specifics, one can easily misread it, get confused or just not have the same idea as was intended by the Author.

Similarly, when people say to "follow Christ" or to "abide in Christ", we need to explain what those terms really mean. We need to explain exactly what is intended. I remember I was sitting in Church one day and the Pastor said "follow Christ" - this was repeated a couple of times but I didn't (at the time) know what "follow Christ" meant. How can I follow through on something when I don't know what it means?

I wondered if I was alone in this and so after the service, I asked some around me: "Do you know what it means when a Pastor says 'follow Christ' but provides no further detail?" The resounding answer from everyone I asked was no. Nobody who had heard this important but unqualified and unexplained message understood what "follow Jesus" meant. Unless you explain to people and you qualify what is meant by "follow Christ", and this is where a person can get into challenging situations. When we don't fully understand what something is supposed to mean or what something is supposed to look like, we can get caught up with wrong interpretations and can get lost trying to understand it. We can fall into wrong and incorrect teachings, which is what I saw and watched happen to many around me.

Through my own primary and secondary research, I found out that this means:

- Take the example of Christ from the Bible - many examples are provided of the kind of Man Jesus was, things He did, wisdom He dispensed, sicknesses He eradicated and more.
- Support organizations that explicitly support Christ.
- Use Christ's awesome examples of care, healing, compassion, empathy, kindness and much more.
- Respect the Word of God the way that Christ did. Listen carefully to the instructions provided and follow those instructions carefully and to the letter.
- Pray regularly. One of the greatest tools we have ever been given is to pray regularly to Jesus, through the Holy Spirit. This, just like Jesus did, is our opportunity to honor Christ, to thank Him for all the good things, to ask for those things we would like, to use the same tools that Jesus used in the Bible, and much more.
- Love and respect Christ-centered Churches that teach and explain based on the Bible's teachings. I want to make it clear here that any building can put a cross up on its roof and call itself a Church, but a Church that follows Christ will uphold all of God's teachings.
- Repent (which is a fancier way of saying "say sorry") when you have committed a sin. No sin is too great and no person is beyond help. Repent for what you have done wrong, and then move forward in a fresh, new and healthier way.
- Be obedient - when God shows you something He would like you to do, be obedient and do it. I want to say here that you may not understand all that God is asking you to do - do it anyway. Later,

when you understand what He was doing in your life, you will be happy you followed.

A Loving Relationship

Being a follower of Christ means having a loving relationship with Him. This means an active, daily, vibrant, loving relationship with Him. This is at the heart and is the cornerstone of everything else we do and it is a relationship that has to be nurtured every day. We nurture this relationship in all of the following ways:

- Pray
- Journal
- Engage in times of fellowship with other believers
- Listen to sermons
- Participate in prayer circles for yourself and for others

When we understand Christ and the way the relationship with Him works, we can begin to understand what and why we are being led to something. Without this active, loving and vibrant relationship, we are not sure if we are understanding things correctly and we are simply not sure of our path.

When we have that relationship with Him, it can be easier to be obedient when you get direction and instructions and this is what I will be talking about in the next section.

Being Obedient When You Get Instructions

Being obedient when you get instructions is exactly what it sounds like. When we receive instructions, we get step 1, not steps 1-15. In other words, we will only get instructions for the first step, not all the steps. The next step will be revealed once the first step is completed.

Also, sometimes, we get instructions that may not make sense to us at the time of receipt and so we hesitate to complete the action or because of our uncertainty or the fact that the instructions don't make sense to us, we don't take action. We don't want to appear "out of left field" to others, or we don't want to appear foolish, so we may be nervous or fearful about what taking this step will actually mean. Do it anyway. God has a reason for the instructions He gave you and He gave it to you in the way and at the time that He did for a very good reason. He is looking to see if you will take the first step in obedience, without a full or a good understanding of what that step means or where it will lead. In other words, He is not looking to show you the entire proverbial staircase but instead, for you to take the first step in faith and then let Him lead you to the second step after successful completion of the first.

4

Free Will

We undoubtedly all know that God has given you the free will to choose. He has given each and every one of us the ability to make our own choices and the ability to either obey Him or to not obey Him. He does, of course, hope that you will choose the path He has set for you and that you will follow as He leads.

We do not need to lean on our own understanding of the situation but instead, to trust in Him. What exactly does that mean? It means that He has given you some instructions that may seem strange or foreign to you or instructions that don't make sense to you right now. Do them anyway because He can see things that you can't, He knows things you don't, and He knows what is coming up in the future in a way that you do not.

Here are some examples of some people who stepped out in faith and the resulting outcomes from their faith actions. Names will have been changed. In these outlines of experiences, I will be including some of my own experiences as well because as you may have guessed, I have definitely had to take blind action in faith on many things in my life as well and if I can use examples from my own life to help you, my reader, better understand how God works and how faith and obedience worked together to create blessings, then I have done what I was guided and set out to do.

Blind faith action example 1: A man was guided to go to a certain woman he saw in Church and to give her the money he had in his pocket. He did not know the woman or have any previous interaction with her, so this felt like a bit of a strange request he felt he was getting from the Lord. He wasn't sure how to do this and so he prayed and asked God (in his mind) to make this more clear and for an explanation. The answer that came continued to be to just go up to the woman and to give her the money he had in his pocket. The man felt terribly awkward and wasn't sure how he was going to fulfill the request but he did as he was told. After the service, the man discreetly went over to the woman and told her that he felt led to give her the money he had in his pocket, $50. As he was handing the bill over to the woman, he waited for her reaction and she tearfully accepted the money, explaining that she didn't have any money to get herself back home and that her husband had just left her and the kids. She needed the money to pay for bus tickets to get back home to Ottawa for her and the kids after having left the apartment she had shared with her soon-to-be ex-husband. The man in question felt extremely happy that he listened and obeyed the Lord and that he was able to help this woman. He didn't know her and he didn't initially know why he was being guided to help her but that's the thing with blind faith, you are going on the promptings of God to get something accomplished and you likely won't know the reason about it until you have completed the task.

Blind faith action example 2: A woman named Yvette was carrying around her Bible in her bag. She was a regular reader of the Bible and a woman of faith. She was at the grocery store and saw a sweet little old lady who appeared to be looking for something near the bookstore section of the store. She was clearly not finding what she was looking for because she looked like she was getting a little bit frustrated. Yvette decided to gently approach the woman and ask her if she was ok. The old lady looked at her carefully for a moment and said that she had prayed for a certain book to come to her and that the book in question would be near the books section of the store but she felt confounded because she could neither see the book she was looking for, nor did she have much money, so she was wondering how she was going to pay for the book. When Yvette asked her what book it was she was looking for, the old lady said "Well, I'm looking for a student version of the Holy Bible. I don't understand the full version so when I asked God to help me understand, I felt like He was guiding me here but it doesn't make sense. The book is not here and I don't even know how much it would be. I only have just enough to pay for my few groceries here." Yvette felt strongly in her spirit that she was the answer to the old lady's prayers and so she handed her the student Bible she had been carrying around. She reached into her bag and offered it to the old lady, explaining "I'm pretty sure I am meant to give you my student Bible, and I won't accept any money for it. I was meant to notice you in this area and come over to you. Please accept my student Bible and enjoy it." The old lady was standing there, jaw dropped. She didn't realize that when God said the book would be near the bookshelves, that He didn't mean it would be on the actual shelf, but that the book would come to her near the shelving area. This is just another example of how God works - we are expecting to access the blessing in one way but God will bring it to us in His special way.

Blind faith action example 3: Josh went for an interview at a company. The position seemed perfect for him. It was right up his professional alley. He fulfilled all the position education and experience requirements, and the company was located near his home. He was also having a great interview with the boss so he felt this was perfect for him. Still, when he prayed about it, he felt that something was wrong. He came to consult with me about the uneasiness he was feeling and I advised him that if something feels off, that is the Holy Spirit speaking to him, telling him something is not as it seems and to do with the situation as he felt guided. During the interview, everything seemed fine, including the man who interviewed him, who seemed to have a great head on his shoulders and seemed genuinely interested in what Josh would be bringing to the role. The interview went way into overtime because the two seemed to be professionally connecting. Still, something seemed off. I advised Josh to pray that God would make clear what was feeling so off and then to wait patiently for the answer. Josh ended up not getting the job and he was totally confused and perplexed by this development, but even when he contacted the man with whom he had interviewed, there was no reply. A couple of weeks later, Josh found out that the company had been involved in some shady deals and that they were undergoing a federal investigation, and that the company was facing being shut down for tax evasion. Had Josh gotten that job, he would have been linked to that and his department would have actually been the one who would have had to answer for that, new as he would have been and unfamiliar with the situation as he would have been. Instead, a friend ended up telling Josh about another job that was also in the same field, at another company. Josh applied to that job and was immediately hired.

Blind faith action example 4: A Pastor I know was finishing up with a pre-covid business trip and couldn't wait to get to bed, knowing that he had a very early flight the next morning. As he was finally getting to bed, exhausted as can be, he felt nudgings in his spirit to get up and pray. Out of sheer exhaustion and a desperate need for some shut-eye, he wanted to ignore the promptings but it kept coming again and again, "Johnny, get up and pray." After ignoring the promptings a couple more times, he finally asked "Why do I have to get up and pray....why can't someone else this time?" and the reply came swiftly, "Because something is wrong with your plane and you need to pray about it." This time, the Pastor got up, knelt by the bed and began to pray in his half-sleepy state. As he climbed back into bed, the Lord spoke to him again and said "Pray for Me to do what I need to do in order to get that plane to be safe and not claim any lives." Deeply frustrated from exhaustion but willing to comply for his life and the lives of other passengers, he prayed this prayer and then got about 1 hour of sleep. When he presented himself at the gate where the flight would be boarding, everything seemed normal at first, and the flight was still scheduled to proceed as usual. Within minutes, though, an announcement came from one of the attendants, explaining that a routine maintenance check had been completed and that part of the plane was found to not be up to standard. The attendant announced that they would be calling for a new (safer) plane to be flown in and that the flight would be delayed about 30 minutes. Despite his original flight being delayed, Johnny felt a great sense of happiness and peace in his spirit because he knew that his prayer had caused the defect to be detected and for another plane to transport him and his fellow passengers safely.

Blind faith action example 5: Tana was driving in the family car when she felt a very strong urge to go to the mechanic and to have the car inspected. She did not understand this prompting at all because she had recently gotten an oil change done and the car was in very good shape. On top of that, she knew she was driving one of the most reliable brands of cars on the market. Still, the urge persisted as she continued with her day and her many errands that day. I recall her telling me that she had so much to do, she really didn't have time to take the car to the mechanic but I too got a sense that she should take the car in. Eventually, she relented and took the car to a nearby mechanic and explained to them that she sensed something was wrong with the car. The mechanic took the car in to inspect it and within 15 minutes, concluded that the car had been leaking oil and had she continued to drive the car as-is, that she was putting herself in serious danger because a fire could have erupted at any time and caused an explosion because the leak was near a gauge on the bottom of the car. Tana was taken completely aback. Because she had already taken the car in for another issue just a little while before that, she had assumed that everything was fine with the car, and seeing as it was running normally, she didn't think twice about it. Had she continued to drive the car as-is, concluded the mechanic, there would have been a strong chance of it having caught fire because the location of the leak made it more vulnerable to a fire. Tana was so grateful that she had decided to listen to the nudgings, instead of ignoring them and relying on her own understanding.

Blind faith action example 6: This next example will hopefully help show how blind faith can turn someone's life around completely. In one day, Bob's life changed completely. He was a happily married tech consultant in Canada, with two children and a dog. He felt that everything was perfect and he was happy with everything he had built in his life. Until everything changed. Over the course of the day, Bob got into a car accident and was rushed to the hospital for emergency surgery. As he was awakening from his surgery, he was feeling very angry with God for having put him through that and having allowed him to get into a life-threatening car accident. He was also surprised that when he woke up in the hospital, neither his wife nor his children were there by his side. When he asked the hospital staff if his wife had been contacted after his accident, the hospital confirmed that she had been contacted but that she had not shown up. No phone calls, nothing. Even his two children were not around. Bob became very angry and when he was released from the hospital a few days later, as he was deemed well enough to go home and take care in the comfort of his home, he got home and found that all of his wife's clothes and belongings were no longer there, nor were the belongings of his children. Only the dog was left there. Bob was extremely confused and the only explanation he got was days later, via an email from his wife explaining that she did not feel that the marriage had been working or that he was good enough for her. She called him a loser in the email and explained that she had not only taken the kids away, but that she did not feel the need to go to the hospital to be there for him since she was ending the marriage. Bob's world was spinning around him and he didn't know what to do. He thought that everything had been fine. When I spoke to him, he indicated that during many instances in his marriage, he had sensed that something was not right and that his wife was not being completely honest with him and recalled hearing sermons in passing about turning your life over to God. He had dismissed all notions of having a relationship with God because he considered himself to be an atheist. Later, he found out that his wife had been having affairs, that she had been poisoning their kids' minds with lies about their dad, and that she had actually remortgaged the house without telling him and had walked away with lots of money. Bob was totally perplexed and realized that he had been living a lie. After a period of depression, Bob found himself turning to God for help. He wanted his children back and he was in dire financial straits. Over the course of a couple of years, Bob began learning about God and the beauty found in relationship with Him. He learned how to turn his life over to God and that next time, he needed to follow the promptings of the Holy Spirit when he was being nudged that something was not right. Since then, Bob has done an incredible job of turning things around for himself and following the prompts of God. Today, he regularly attends a Bible-based Church, he has met a new woman that God brought into his life, his finances are now in order and while it was difficult, he now has a healthy relationship with his children.

Blind faith example 7: Robert felt drawn to Lize. She was his co-worker so he didn't feel it was right to pursue things, lest things don't go well and then they would have what he termed "an awkward office situation" but he felt inexplicably drawn to her. Robert was a man of faith and he prayed over the situation many times, asking God to take away his feelings for Lize if these romantic feelings were not from Him. Weeks turned into months and again and again, Robert continued to feel drawn to Lize. At this point, he had people in his parish who were encouraging him to go for it with Lize. All the signs were pointing to this being a great and exciting new possibility and he and Lize were also friends who got along great. Finally one day, Robert decided he would take the first step that he felt he was being guided to take. He asked Lize to get together for dinner. They had never had dinner before, only coffee and only as friends. As soon as he asked her to dinner, Lize smiled and looked surprised. She accepted his invitation. At dinner, they began to talk about their mutual workplace, their enjoyment of their friendship and many other things. It was becoming clear that they were hitting it off as romantic prospects as much as they had always hit it off as friends. Robert felt the evening called for a little "move" and so he leaned in to kiss Lize for the first time. Fireworks! They realized that their friendship had grown into something much more and that they were starting to fall for each other. Fast forward to today and Robert and Lize are married with four children. When asked about this in hindsight, Robert says that he is very glad he listened to the promptings of the Holy Spirit and that he took the first step in causing the evolving of his friendship with Lize. Today, he is very grateful for their marriage which has at its base, a solid friendship.

I hope you will take from these examples that God wants a relationship with you and that He wants this so that He can provide you with salvation, He can guide you to His best for your life and so that He may have a loving relationship with you. Your definition of best and His may not line up but you don't want to rely on your own definition because we cannot see and understand the true context of things. We operate with flawed, human minds. He operates with a perfect, flawless mind. We are supposed to rely on Him to help us and to open the right doors at the right time.

5

God Will Bring It...But We Have to Ask & Listen

Every person has dreams on their heart, things they would like, and God is the One who will bring each person all of these good things and will bring each person faith and guidance and help, no matter where you are, who you are, what you have done, how far gone you think you are, etc. Visualizing those things each day and seeing mental images both in front of you (tangibly) and in your mind (intangibly) is a necessary way to bring those things to come to pass.

Visualizing

Visualizing means seeing in the eyes of your mind the great things God wants to bring you via images provided by the Holy Spirit. It means to focus the eyes of your heart on the images God puts on your heart and to enjoy seeing all the details of that thing.

For example, if you want something (or you think you want something) and you visualize it independently from what God has guided you to, then you are visualizing your own desires, and this has nothing to do with God. If, however, He has put a dream in your heart, He will give you the visuals to help you see it and make it more tangible in your mind.

In the Biblical example of Abraham, Abraham wanted a son. God showed him an image (the sky with the many stars) and used this visual to show Abraham what He was intending to bring him. Abraham hadn't asked for "descendants as numerous as the stars in the sky" - no, he had just asked for a son but God had bigger plans. God's plan was to give Abraham a son in addition to giving him many descendants. The promise Abraham received was for much more than just one son - he would get that son and so much more.

Visualizing according to the information God has given you is key. It gives us a visual representation of what God wants to bless us with and we can access that visual as often and in as much detail as we have been given. Visualizing is as strong and as powerful as prayer. When we visualize based on what He has put on our heart, it communicates to Him that we also want what He plans to give us and that we are working on achieving that through the steps He inspires us to take.

> **Every dream we are given requires strategic, inspired action. If we do not take strategic action, then that thing is not likely to come to pass because everything requires strategic and inspired actions in order to manifest.**

To be clear: every dream we are given requires strategic, inspired action. If we do not take strategic actions, then that thing is not likely to come to pass because everything requires strategic and inspired actions in order to manifest. Simply put, it will always just be a dream unless you put strategic, consistent, God-ordered action to it. For example, you can want to be a great doctor but if you don't work diligently toward that by studying hard, taking the right courses, submitting your work on time, working hard to get into a medical school and volunteer and do the internships/residency that are required, then you are not going to get to where you want to be.

You can desire to be a great actress but if you don't take the time to hone your craft, to submit yourself for postings, and to work on building good relationships with others in the industry, it isn't likely to happen.

You can desire to be a very successful mechanic but if you don't work hard in shop class, understanding all the parts of vehicles, how things need to be changed, how to build strategic relationships and how to apply for the appropriate jobs as they come, then you are not going to succeed at what you are aiming for.

Visualizing Is As Good As Action

This is an important point. Science (which was created and invented by God) does tell us that our brains cannot tell the difference between an action performed in our mind and one performed in reality. As such, your brain cannot tell the difference between a lived experience and an imagined experience because even when the experience is imagined, it is real. The human brain can't tell the difference.

This means, therefore, that you can do the very dream or goal that you have in your heart today. You can undertake the actions today and your brain will not be able to tell the difference.

Here are some examples:

- If you want to be a doctor (as in my previous example further up), see in your mind a video (if you will) of yourself being a doctor in the setting that you desire. See all aspects of it and hold those images in your mind for at least 15 minutes.
- If you want to be a best-selling author, see in your mind a video

(if you will) of your books hitting the bestseller list and next to your name, the status of bestselling author.
- If you want to be a dedicated parent, see the video in your mind of you taking care of your child or children, being there for them, tending to their needs and of them telling you you're a great parent and how much they appreciate you.
- If you want to be a successful entrepreneur, see yourself at the helm of your business, taking all the decisions necessary for the successful operation of your business, answering the phone calls and the emails and see your revenue streams coming in.
- If you want to be a great employee who makes a great salary, see yourself at your desk, working hard and doing a great job, with your boss telling you he or she is impressed with the work you are doing and how you are close to your next promotion

Your Imagination Is the Only Limiting Factor

Here is another piece of great news: the only limiting factor to your dreams becoming reality is your own. Your own imagination. God has not only given us visions and dreams He has put on our hearts and in our minds but He has also given us the ability to replay and see those dreams actively again and again. When we take the time to see our dreams play out in our minds again and again, it brings that dream to pass much more quickly. How often you see yourself performing your dreams and goals tells Him how much it means to you and how much you are willing to dedicate yourself to its successful pursuit and realization.

As such, we need to make sure that we are visualizing with Jesus at the center of our practice. How do we visualize with Jesus? We do so by asking the Holy Spirit to come into our hearts and to help guide our visuals. To help us see all aspects and details of it more readily and more clearly.

The more you do this, the faster your dreams will come to pass.

6

God Has Already Done His Part. You Already Have It.

Many people mistakenly assume that because they haven't yet received what they want, that God is withholding that good thing from them. Nothing could be further from the truth. God, through His death on the cross, has already done everything, has accomplished everything and has given us everything. Everything you want already exists in the Spirit. Now, we have to do our part and cause it to be "pulled down" to earth. How do we do this? We see (via visualization) the manifestation of that thing on earth.

Here are some Scripture passages to verify this with explanations after each passage:

> **Philippians 4:19** - And my God will supply every need of yours according to his riches in glory in Christ Jesus.

God will supply every need you have and He knows what your needs are better than you do. Also, because He is able to see 365 degrees, He knows exactly what things will be good for you in the long run, not just right now. This is why we need to trust in Him, He who always wants the best for us. Further, when it says "according to His riches", it means that He is going to give us more than we could have fathomed with our human minds.

> **Matthew 7:11 - If you then, who are evil, know how to give good gifts to your children, how much more will your Father who is in heaven give good things to those who ask him!**

People love their children and love to show their children how much they love them. They do this in many ways and since we, as humans, show our children how much we love them, how much more will God show us, His children, how much He loves us with the many beautiful blessings He wants to bring us. This never just means monetary and tangible gifts, but also includes gifts of love, compassion, empathy, being there, being present, sharing love and laughter, and so much more. So, if we humans know how to give good gifts, please know that the Lord knows how to give gifts 1000 times better and takes enjoyment in doing so.

> **Psalm 34:10 - The young lions suffer want and hunger; but those who seek the Lord lack no good thing.**

Those who seek the Lord will not lack anything good because we rely on God's goodness to provide us with those good things. Will everything you want or desire come exactly when you want or desire it?

Likely not. But we have to remain grateful for all that He has given us and we can certainly ask for things we do not yet have.

> **Jeremiah 29:11 - For I know the plans I have for you, declares the Lord, plans for welfare and not for evil, to give you a future and a hope.**

If you are a person who is hurting today or even if you are not, know that God has wonderful plans for you, plans that are intended to give you a good future and good wealth and health. But, you do need to follow Him and His instructions in order to access all those good things.

In general, if we don't follow Him, know Him and understand Him, how can He be expected to bring us all those good things?

Think About It....He Has Already Provided

God has already provided for us in so many ways. He provided Jesus (Savior of all who believe in Him), He provided the world, nature, and all the provisions of the earth. He provided us with life, love, happiness, the ability to think and to reason, He provided fresh air and breath and the list goes on and on. If we already know this about Him, why would He withhold any good thing from us?

The simple answer is: He doesn't.

Now, He may not yet have brought you everything you wanted. That is not because He is being mean or trying to withhold good things from you but rather, any of the following reasons could apply as to why you have not yet received what you have wanted:

- The timing of it is not right yet

- The person or people involved are not ready yet
- You haven't prayed for it yet
- What you have asked for is not the right thing for you
- You don't believe you will actually get it
- God is looking to change you so that you are ready for that gift

Faith As Small As a Mustard Seed

We talk about belief a lot. Believing and faith go hand-in-hand. When we believe, we have faith. In the Bible, it says faith as small as a mustard seed will be needed to make wonderful things happen. But what does that actually mean? It means that even a little bit of faith can take you a very long way. God knew that as humans, we would be making some errors and that sometimes, we would not be strong in our faith due to mishaps, disappointments, delays, wrong turns, etc. That's why it says that all you need is faith as small as a mustard seed to cause good things to happen for you. It is very important to realize and recognize that this is another provision that God is making to help us, to support us and to allow us to access His goodness via limited faith and within the given context of our flawed nature.

Someone asked me long ago: *"Christine, may I pray for more faith?"* She was asking me if she may pray for God to give her more faith. Certainly! We can and we should pray for Him to give us more faith. You see, God is so powerful and He controls everything so He is able to change us from the inside out. This is a very important point: God is so powerful that He can change us and anyone else from the inside out. It does not mean that you change people. That won't work. You can pray for God to change a person and if it's right, He will. Can we visualize God changing people? Yes, we can. Visualizing is another form of praying and creating so when we pray to the Ultimate Creator, yes, we are in fact asking Him to change that person...and He does, as long as it benefits the person and changes them positively. Allow me to illustrate: I will never forget one woman who was telling me about how she wanted to change her husband. She was coming at it from a place of wanting him to be different in things and in ways that given his current ways, bothered her. Well, she was being a bit selfish on this and so God convicted her on that point. Instead, He changed her heart on the matter and helped her see that she needed to pray for things that would benefit him.

An example of praying for another person for their improvement can be any of the following (and this is not an exhaustive list):

- Praying for someone to beat an addiction
- Praying for someone to improve their communication with you
- Praying for someone to spend more time with you
- Praying for someone to realize that they did you wrong
- Praying for someone to make amends
- Praying for a person to have good fortune and good blessings in their lives
- Praying for a person to have a closer relationship with God
- Praying for a person to begin praying for themselves and for others
- Praying for a person to want to better themselves and to be more successful in their lives

God Knows Our Hearts

God knows each of us intimately and well. He knows our hearts and our intentions. I remember when, many years ago, I was angry at a former romantic partner, and so I began praying for not such great things to happen to him. The Lord immediately convicted me and told me how wrong I was in praying for that. Instead, what He did is He began to work on me. He began to show me that I needed to pray for this man to actually come to God and to have a relationship with Him so that He could change him, not for my revenge purposes (I know now how wrong this initial prayer was).

God knows each of our hearts and when we hear that "God will meet you where you are", He means it. He will meet you where you are and will help you, no matter what you are currently dealing with and He will guide you to His best, no matter where you are in life. I also want to point out that it is very important for even those people who do not know the Lord well that they can still visualize and partake in this form of prayerful meditation. God welcomes this from everyone but you are reminded to ensure that these are things that God has put on your heart.

How Do I Know If God Put This on My Heart?

This is an important question and there are some simple ways to do this:

1. Ask the Holy Spirit (the Truth Teller) to speak to your heart and to let you know if this desire is from God.
2. Is the desire consistent with Scripture? If you are asking if it is God's will for you to hurt someone, I can tell you straight up and right now that that is not God's will. He calls for us to love our neighbor and to not kill or destroy.
3. Pray for clarity and for Him to give you vision about this.

7

The Right Way and the Wrong Way

There is a right way to manifest and a wrong way to manifest. Simply put.

I'd like to give an example here of something not being right for you because this is one point many people I have spoken to wonder about. A man I was romantically interested long ago and sensed that he, too, was interested in me, started flirting with me. He flirted quite a bit and I was definitely growing more and more "into him". I prayed over the situation many times and each time, I sensed God say that this man was not right for me. Each time I asked, I sensed the same answer again and again. I became a bit frustrated because to my human mind, there seemed no logical reason for this "no" answer. So, I spent time in quiet meditation to think about it. Through the promptings of the Holy Spirit, I began to see and understand little moments where this man showed me different parts of his feelings and his character. I began to realize more than more that while he displayed an interest in me, he displayed a much greater one for another woman we both knew. Upon looking at this situation with the Holy Spirit's wisdom, I began to see how he had fallen for the other woman and was just too afraid to tell me that he liked her more than me. I was distraught for a while but then I was able to pull myself out of it. It really helped to spend that time with the Truth-Teller. Simply and frankly, I was not really seeing the full picture. Today, that man and that lady are happily married.

Not every path is the right one for you and we need to be cognizant and respectful enough of God's wisdom and goodness to recognize that when He guides us away from something, it is for our own best interest and His will. Remember what I had said further up: He is not looking to withhold good things from you so when He does guide you away from something, know that it is because it is not the best thing for you.

It Appears Good

Bad things don't necessarily present themselves as being bad for you. Even bad things can and likely will be cloaked in "good" appearance but when we look further into it, when we probe and we check, we can see that there are indicators that it will not be good for us. I take the example here of Donna. Donna was presented with interest from a handsome man who found her on social media and told her how striking he thought she was. Donna had been praying for a spouse so she assumed that this was an answer to her prayer. She began talking to him very casually, telling him little but important things about her, in a bid to let him know more about her and asked him a bit about himself to get to know him a little better. Things seemed to be going wonderfully and at every possible opportunity, this man complimented her and told her how he found qualities of hers to be wonderful. During her prayers, she sensed some uneasiness. She prayed more deeply and it seemed that the Holy Spirit was not calling this a great situation. Donna wisely paid attention to the warnings and upon further probing and following up on little leads, discovered that this man was in fact married and was misrepresenting himself to her. This was clearly the wrong path cloaked as a good possibility.

Are You Ready for The Gift?

I want to ask you a bit about this point: are you ready for the gifts God wants to bring you? God is looking to change you so that you are ready for that gift. You see, many people assume that they are ready today for the receipt of their gift. They think they deserve to have it today, no questions asked. I know this because I felt that way and when I wasn't getting what I wanted right away, it didn't make sense to me. I realized (upon much reflection) that I had to change my outlook a fair bit because there were many things about me that would not have been conducive to receiving and keeping that which I desired. For example, when it comes to becoming a great author, I assumed that I already had the skills to understand the industry and how things would work. I was wrong. Because I was new to the industry, there was a huge learning curve both in writing my books and in publishing my books. I was also a very impatient person and so when things were not happening on my timeline, I was getting upset and unhappy. I wasn't taking the time to review my books, to edit them further, to find out how to use the new publishing platform properly and I (arrogantly) assumed that people would just buy my books or seek them out, and that I didn't have to work on marketing or promoting my books in any way. Simply put: people didn't know me yet and I overlooked that a connection first needs to be made with people before anything else happens. I also needed to better understand my audience and how to deliver to them the Word of God, my experiences, and to show them how my experiences can be of benefit to them. I had a lot to learn and the Lord humbled me many times to learn those things.

> **I also needed to better understand my audience and how to deliver to them the Word of God, my experiences, and to show them how my experiences can be of benefit to them.**

I also assumed that when it comes to marriage, that my husband and I would just meet, fall in love, get married and that's it. I didn't stop to think of whether I had yet developed the skills to be married because marriage requires a certain set of skills in order to work well. You can have a marriage without those skills but it doesn't mean it will be a good or a healthy marriage. I realized upon deep reflection that I needed to develop all of the following skills in order to be married successfully and to show my (future) husband unconditional love: unconditional love, self-sacrifice, spending time praying for him, for me and for us (as opposed to just praying for myself), being a great listener, being a careful speaker, to be more understanding, to be more giving of my time, and much more.

It took many hours of listening to sermons on successful, Christ-centered marriages and reading about how to cherish my spouse for me to realize that I actually didn't have a clue how to show him my unconditional love. I needed to visualize what a happy marriage would look like, what listening to him and his problems would look like, how doing that would take time away from other things I enjoyed doing (but was still worth it), and what putting him and his needs first would look like.

I was speaking with a friend of mine whom I will name Nan. Nan claimed to me over and over again how she loved the new guy who had come into her life, named Bob and how she felt he was her soulmate. I too felt that he was her soulmate. She said she loved him unconditionally and I wondered what that looked like to her. She explained that it meant putting his needs before her own and being there for him no matter what. I thought it was such a lovely thing when I heard it and I resolved that instead of doubting her, that I would give her an opportunity to show that unconditional love over time. I also suggested some good resources to her where she could learn to develop those skills (because I think everyone could use more help to do that - we are all works in progress). A year passed and she remained dedicated to Bob. I was impressed. I encouraged her to visualize her life with him, married to him, and all that that would look like for her. I encouraged her to see their wedding day, their married life, and the children she had expressed a hope in having one day and I explained to her what I am explaining to you in this book - how this phenomenon helps things to actually happen.

After some time, she began expressing how she loved him but that she had been feeling exhausted praying for him, seeing their married life together but not seeing enough progress. I reminded her that they had both progressed a fair amount and that good things take time to come. I will fast forward a few months later and she announced to me that she was deciding to walk away from him, because she wasn't seeing enough progress quickly enough. I reminded her that unconditional love necessarily means to put the other person first and that in this case, she needed to put Bob's needs first because he had already made some really good changes in life. She was seeing really good changes taking place in his life and was seeing the fruits of her prayers. I encouraged her many times to keep going and that things were moving along. Ultimately, Nan decided to leave it alone, to let it go. Today, they have both moved on to other people and Nan has stopped praying entirely.

When we visualize, we are taking action in the Spirit realm to accomplish bringing to manifest what God has put in our heart. Again, God has provided everything for us. It is all available to us in the spirit realm. Now we have to use the tools of faith and visualization to see those things brought to us in reality.

 Taking a moment to reflect: I'd like to give you a chance here to think about and reflect on something you may have taken for granted in assuming that you were or are ready for it and maybe how you need to be better prepared for it. Feel free to take your journal to write this out. Remember to put it somewhere you know you will be able to access it again because you will one day want to look back on this and use it as a further reflective piece and to see how far you have come.

8

Strategic Actions

Taking strategic action is so important. Just because something exists in the Spirit, it does not mean that we will see it immediately in real life. We have to work at that and we need to take the necessary actions to come to see what we envision to pass.

For example, you can want to be a millionaire (and that's great) but only visualizing it will not be enough to produce the desired outcome. You have to work hard and strategically to accomplish this - the money is not going to just drop into your lap. Even if you want to win the lottery and become a millionaire that way, fine, but you have to go out and buy the lottery ticket and pick the right numbers. The fulfillment of every dream comes with strategic, decisive and consistent action.

3 Steps

The following are the three steps that show how, done properly and consistently, can be applied over and over again for the achievement of any dream, wish or desire:

1. Sit down in a comfortable place, quiet your mind and ask the Holy Spirit to open you up to being able to see and visualize the way that God wants you to.
2. In quiet concentration and focus, visualize and focus the eyes of your heart to experiencing the reality of being in actual possession of that dream, making it super real in your mind's eye and your heart, feeling all the feelings you would if that dream were accomplished right now, in reality, meditating on the reality of having already received it in your mind. Spend time feeling the feelings of happiness and elation as you are performing the actions of your dreams and goals.
3. Pray for God to tell you which strategic actions will be needed for the attainment and realization of that goal. Ask Him to speak to you about the ways He wants and the time frame that He is guiding you to

Here are some examples of how the three-step concept can be applied:

Example 1

If you are a single person looking to meet and marry your God-given spouse, take some time each day to:

1) Quiet your mind and invite the Holy Spirit to open up your mind and the eyes of your heart to this new blessing.

2) See yourself experiencing and being right now in possession of what you were seeking and

3) Ask God to show you what steps are needed for you to meet that person and come together in a committed, monogamous and exclusive relationship with that person.

Example 2

If you are looking for a new job:

1) Ask the Holy Spirit to guide you and to help make this visual so real

2) Visualize yourself in the new job, doing all the actions that that new job would entail, making the experience as real for yourself as possible and

3) Ask God to show you what specific steps will be needed for you to take in order to land the job God has prepared for you and for you to be extremely successful in the position

Example 3

If the medical report is not good and you would like to see and feel yourself being completely healed:

1) Ask the Holy Spirit to guide you and to help make this visual so real

2) Visualize yourself being completely healed, with the Holy Spirit's power taking away any sickness and any disease from your body, and making the experience as real for yourself as possible. See yourself as already being in great health, and see the medical report being changed to one of a clean bill of health.

3) Ask God to show you what specific steps will be needed for you to take in order to get that clean bill of health and invite His healing powers to completely restore perfect health unto you

Example 4

If you are looking to mend a relationship, any kind of relationship:

1) Invite the Holy Spirit to help you see this relationship mended.

2) Visualize yourself experiencing the mended version of the relationship, experiencing in detail all that that new relationship would bring with it and

3) Ask God to show you what steps would be needed in order to take strategic action on how to mend that relationship.

Example 5

If you are looking to become a better community member and to give more of yourself to others via volunteer work or otherwise:

1. Invite the Holy Spirit to help you see where you should be spending your time and your energy
2. Visualize yourself doing the good works with an organization that the Lord is leading you to help, seeing yourself taking sample actions like sorting, organizing, serving, and being a helpful community member. Remember that just because you visualize yourself in one particular area, it does not mean that that is definitely the area within which you will be serving. For example, you can see yourself as the person sorting food that has been donated to the charity, but it doesn't mean that that's the area where you will definitely be used. Visualizing it is a powerful way of getting the door to be opened for you to doing something to help that charity. If you desire a specific function within an organization, you can focus on that and when the time comes to voice where you would like to participate, you can state that function as being the one you desire.
3. Ask God to show you which charity would be the right one to help and what steps would be needed in order to take strategic action to help that charity.

You Might Be Surprised

One thing in particular that I would like to mention here is that when you pray for direction, you may get a very different answer than the one you thought you would. For example, a person can wish to volunteer and lend support to their local Church but they need to pray to see if that is where God wants them to dedicate their time and energy. Allow me to explain: just because an organization calls itself a

Church, it doesn't mean that that will automatically get the green light for where you will be helping. Not every place that calls itself a Church is actually doing the right works and holding true to Biblical values. Also, just because an organization is considered a registered charity, it doesn't mean that's where the Lord will have you work. For example, there was an event happening at a local Church that I was invited to attend and participate in but when I prayed about it, I got a very clear answer to not go to or attend that event. It didn't mean there was something not right about the event (it was a great event being presented by a good, Bible-based Church that I still consider myself to be a member of) but the Lord wanted my time to be spent elsewhere. In fact, I discovered (upon not going to the event) that I would be staying home and working on one of the manuscripts I had written but not yet published at that time.

God is very particular about how He wants us to spend our time. He is a very strategic God and wants us to spend our time in the right places, doing the right things according to His will. So, when you do make time to visualize, make sure you check with Him that you are putting your efforts and energy in the right place. After all, it is work and it does take dedication and commitment to do what you need to do to bring about the results that we need to bring forth.

9

Vision Boards

Vision boards are a wonderful and an often misunderstood tool in some circles. Because they are used and touted by non-Christian belief systems, Christians immediately think they should be running away from them. They shouldn't be. Vision boards are a concept given to us by God and are a visual representation that we can use to keep our God-given goals in front of us, reminding us to do what we need to do to achieve those goals. The visual depiction helps us by providing us with a reminder to begin or to continue to take action toward the fulfillment of that goal. Keeping the name of Jesus at the center of your vision board is both wise and recommended.

Vision boards are a fantastic tool that each person can use to keep their goals front and center, in the midst of the many other things they need to do. They can be used by anyone at any time to show us a visual of what we need to do to achieve our goals. I would also like to point out that words on your vision board are a great idea too because we then get a short reminder of one word or phrase to ensure that we are on-task and on-target.

> Vision boards are a visual representation that we can use to keep our goals in front of us, reminding us to do what we need to do to achieve those goals. The visual depiction helps us by providing us with a reminder to begin or to continue to take action toward the fulfillment of that goal.

One thing I would strongly suggest to include on your vision board are the words: The will of Father God, Jesus and the Holy Spirit. Why? Because this will help serve as an additional reminder that the goals that you have set for yourself and that are in front of you are God's will and that you are honoring God's will by including His name onto your board. This will also certainly help differentiate your board and will demonstrate that you are honoring Christ with it.

What Can I Put On My Vision Board

Include on your vision board anything and everything that helps make the visual depiction of your goal as real for you as possible. As I was scouring different resources, here are some examples that I found that I thought were truly interesting. You may or may not want to take note of how these people did theirs and of course, you are welcome to select some items from theirs to make your board if you believe it speaks to you.

Here are some examples of vision boards:

Vision Board

Seeing It Again and Again

Part of the power of vision boards is your ability and benefit to see the visual representations again and again. Seeing something once is helpful but seeing it again and again is so much more helpful and allows it to serve as a consistent reminder to you to take consistent action. Also, and this is especially important, when you have your vision board and goals in front of you, you will need to use the encouragement, the reminders and the motivation to keep going despite the obstacles and challenges that you will face. Everybody experiences challenges, and experiences difficulties - it is what we do in the face of those challenges that inspire greatness and that inspire us to see beyond the difficulties. After all, if you managed to achieve your goals in no time at all and without having overcome challenges, would that really be a much-valued and deeply-desired item? In the words of the great Michael Phelps, "Would it really be that much fun and that great if we always got what we wanted without trying and with ease?" Mr. Phelps put it perfectly: part of what makes the attainment and the achievement of the goal so valuable is the fact that we have to work very hard and sustain much in order to be granted the recipient of the goal.

One of the things I used to ask my students to do at the beginning of the year was to ask them to create and to put up posters of all shapes, colors and sizes to use as motivation, encouragement and reminders during the year to persevere and to keep going when things get challenging later in the year, whether in their studies, their extra-curriculars or their personal lives. Each student was responsible for at least one poster and to take ownership of that poster throughout the year, so that they have that ownership-responsibility of their encouraging reminder. My intent and my hope with this was that all the students will not only mentally prepare themselves for the inevitable upcoming challenges but that this was also a means to help them face those challenges with encouragement head-on when they do present themselves. The ownership portion of it was helpful for those students who may have been a little less motivated and so ownership of their poster necessarily meant that they would care at least about their poster and would serve as a reminder to themselves.

Put The Reminders All Around

Some people only put up one vision board. You can do that but it may very well be more effective if you put up vision boards or at least helpful reminders all over your room, your home, your vehicle, etc. This will allow for consistent reminders as you go through each part of your day and not when you are just in the room where you put the original board.

Seeing the visuals again and again is a tremendous reminder of your goals and the fact that you will need to take tremendous amounts of action to attain them. Further, it is really important to see the visuals again and again so that they get lodged into your subconscious, further helping to cause you to think about these all the time.

Your Vision Board

I'd like to give you an opportunity at this point in the book to think about what you would like to see up on your vision board. Think about all aspects of it, from the pictures and words you would like to use to the dimensions.

Use the space provided here to jot down your ideas:

10

Live It!

    Many people often ask me what would be a major help to manifesting? A major help would be the ability to believe that we have already achieved it and we need to act as though we have already achieved it!

    When you have achieved something that you have wanted, it is natural for people to feel excited, elated, have a tremendous sense of accomplishment and be able to stand up tall because they have accomplished what they want. When you are manifesting a promise, that's the feeling that you need to remind yourself that you already have it because that is what brings about the blessing. When we imagine ourselves as having already accomplished something, things begin to work in our favor and things begin to happen for us because God is working on our behalf and making sure that the full promise is completed. So when you act as though you've already got it, what you are doing is honoring and helping the work that the Lord is doing in your life and in the lives of others who are needed to cause the manifestation of that blessing. We have to remember that believing we have it is vital to the process and that when we can see it with all the detail possible, so vividly in our mind and in our hearts, then you know that it is done and only a matter of time before you see it manifest in real life.

It is the same process and takes the same amount of energy to manifest something small as it would take for something bigger. For example, it takes the same amount of time, effort, and energy to manifest $10 as it would take to manifest $10,000. Another example is that it would take the same amount of time to manifest complete health as it would take to manifest the renewing of a relationship. Many people are often under the impression that the bigger things will take longer to manifest. That is not so. The only thing that we are waiting for is for God to line up everything properly and perfectly in our life and the lives of those around us. While you are waiting, the currency of faith and the belief that you will receive the manifestation is what helps you to hold to that promise and to have faith that it is on its way to you. When we manifest, we are demonstrating our faith in what the Lord is able to do and using the tools that he has provided for us. This is not something that we are doing separately from the Lord. Quite the contrary. Doing this honors the infrastructure that He has already put in place within every single one of us and brings to life all that he wants for us!

I will use some two-way journaling here to give you a sense of what the Holy Spirit is saying about this here:

Me: Holy Spirit, is everything I am saying so far accurate and true? What do You want to say to people through me?

H.S.: You are speaking truthfully. Manifesting is one of the greatest tools the Lord Jesus has given to people. Anyone can do it anywhere but one must keep his or her eyes firmly on Jesus. Why? Because He is the One who will bring this to pass. He is the One who is working and setting up things perfectly in an effort to bring the manifestation to you. God has instilled visuals, images, proverbs and manifestation as tools that you can use to bring about His perfect will on earth. You,

Christine, have already seen this happen in many ways and in many different contexts. If you visualize, you will see the manifestation come to pass. If you don't visualize, you are making life more difficult for yourself and I think you will agree that life has enough difficulties all on its own.

Me: Thank You. What else do You want to say here?

H.S.: Visualizing is God's original idea. It is His original plan to bring His blessings to humans. When people engage in it, He has the legal right to bring those blessings to pass. When people don't engage in it, it makes everything a thousand times more difficult and God cannot (legally) work to bring about the good things He desires. So important to do so. And vision boards are such beautiful things. Keep the dream in front of you. God created you to be a visual person.

Get In Your Car And Go. Wear The Clothes. Pretend Like It Is.

Want that job? Get in your car in the morning and pretend to drive to that job.

Want the engagement ring? See and feel yourself wearing it and feel what it is like to play with it on that special ring finger.

How about that baby you have been wanting? Go to the store and start buying baby clothes and things for the baby.

A better relationship with a loved one? Add their number on your phone and begin typing a warm and loving message. You don't need to send it but you can type it.

Better health? Begin putting away all the "sick" stuff around the house. Pile them into a closet and tell yourself you don't need any of those things anymore. Why would you!? You are preparing to be in perfect health.

When we believe without a shadow of a doubt and we want to prepare for the manifestation of the promise, we need to live as though

we have it. We need to live as though we are expecting it and it is about to be ours.

I am reminded of the story about a friend of mine who really wanted to marry a very Christian girl that was a good friend in his life but that he didn't feel that she even knew he was alive. I advised him to do exactly this: I advised him to prepare for marriage by reading the Bible, by listening to sermons on how to be a great Christian husband, I urged him to see himself as her husband, and to begin thinking about the kind of engagement ring he would buy for her. He began doing each of these things and fast forward a few months later, and they got engaged, just like he imagined, saw, and prepared for.

This man could very easily have said "No, forget it. It's not worth it or "It's not going to happen," or "She's not interested in me and she never will be", and he could have just left it at that. But if he had done that, where would he be today? He would not be married to her and they would not have had their second child already. When we visualize these things, we signal to God that we have so much faith in what He is doing in His promise that we are preparing for it from now! Don't you want to show God that you have the face to believe from now? If so, begin preparing now.

Infrastructure

I'd like to take a minute to explain infrastructure a little bit more clearly. When I say that God has provided the infrastructure, it means that God has designed us to be able to bring about our dreams and desires. He has built us for this. Scientifically, our minds cannot tell the difference between a perceived lived experience and an actually lived experience. This means that when you see something in your mind and you hold that image for a time, the brain believes that it is actually experiencing it and begins to look for ways to actually make it a reality.

To give you an example: a person who would like to manifest total health in their bodies but whose current health report is terrible can spend some time seeing themselves and feeling completely and totally healthy and of sound mind and body and our entire system will begin to find ways to bring that to reality. God is also working with us to support what we are seeing in our imaginations because remember that He wants the best for us, always. The desire that you have in your heart is a desire that He has given you. How do I know that? Because I have spent an extraordinary amount of time in quiet with the Lord and in ensuring that my walk with Him is as solid as can be. So I know that it is His character to always want the best for us and is not looking to withhold from us. This is why He has provided us with the infrastructure in our bodies so that we can cause the support mechanism to allow Him to do this work within us and within the lives of other people around us. Do you need to have the boss on your side to get that promotion? You do not. If it is the Lord's will and you have spent time visualizing it, the Lord will find a way to bring that blessing to you. Does the doctor's report currently have to read that you are in perfect health for you to begin believing and feeling like you are in perfect health? Certainly not. You can begin to feel it, sense it, and internalize complete health in all parts of your system and things will begin to flow in that direction.

It's almost like saying that when we take the time to visualize and we take the time to put into practice those things that God has given us as tools, He honors us and gets to work on our behalf to make the accomplishments and the realization of that thing a reality. I have come to experience over and over again How He blesses people and how He brings the manifestation when people take the time and put in the effort to practice this.

Eyes Open? Eyes Closed?

One of the questions that I have asked in my own visualization practice is the following: do we need to visualize with our eyes open or closed? I have come to realize that it doesn't matter. As long as what we are seeing complements that goal or that desire in our minds, making it real in our own minds and hearts, then it doesn't matter if we are visualizing with our eyes closed or open.

Wow!

In past practice, when I have asked people to engage in this practice and then asked them how they felt after undertaking the practice, they have consistently said "Wow!" They indicated feeling a shift in their mind and in their life and they began to see things very differently. That's when you know it is working!

Try this for a moment and see your experience with it. Ask the Holy Spirit to highlight in your mind one of your goals or dreams, and take a moment right now to visualize it with your eyes either open or closed, asking the Holy Spirit to make the visual as real and as vivid for you as possible. Think about all the details about it, seeing it as a three-dimensional fact already in your life, imagining how it feels right now, in this moment to possess it. Open the eyes of your heart to see all aspects of it, see it with all the detail you can imagine and hold onto the 3-dimensional image of it for as long as you can.

Take a moment right now to write down how and what you experienced with this exercise:

_____
_____
_____
_____
_____
_____
_____
_____

11

5 Keys To Manifesting Successfully

Here are 5 keys to manifesting successfully:

1. **Be Clear**: Once you have decided what God wants you to manifest, be clear about it and focus on it. Try not to focus on what you don't want. Positive attracts positive. Focus on your desire in a positive light.
2. **Be Consistent**: No matter what it is that you are looking to manifest, ensure that it is consistent. Don't keep changing it drastically. Of course, small tweaks are fine but if you are changing the overall picture fairly regularly, you are not giving it the time it needs to gel.
3. **Trust God and Chill**: This is your opportunity to really trust that your passion and desire are put out there. When the time is right, everything will fall into place. Trusting that God has your back and that He will bring it in His perfect timing.
4. **Take Strategic and Inspired, God-Led Action**: Merely thinking about your desire will not allow it to manifest. Pray to see what God is guiding you to do for the physical manifestation of it and

then...take action! There is no other way but to work towards your vision.

5. **Make Space**: Making space for something new in your life may mean that you need to get rid of the old. This may mean throwing away your old boyfriend's leftover stuff may be important for when your new man comes into your life. Or, letting go of your former girlfriend's memorabilia to make room for the new memorabilia will be important. If you are asking to get into medical school, make room in your life for that to happen, such as making space on your desk for the inevitable barrage and overtaking of books, manuals, medical supplies and much more.

Don't underestimate the need to make space in your life for what you know God is guiding you to. When we hold onto the old, we are not making space for the new and this can certainly block our blessing or delay it. To give you an example, a gentleman that I know and was ministering to knew the first name of his wife and that she was not going to come to him any other way than through me. He had prayed about this and he knew it to be so. I found it a bit odd when one day when I was out walking, I got the sense that I should warn him that this soon-to-be-coming lady love would be testing him to see his devotion to her but I knew I needed to mention it to him. I did and he said he would pray about it. Sure enough, through one of my conversations with him two to three weeks after that warning, he advised me that he had been on a number of dating sites and that he knew in his heart he needed to get off so that he could make room for this new lady. Shortly afterwards, he advised that he had ended his subscriptions to the dating sites, and had asked the companies in question to delete his profile. He was grasping this concept: you have to close that door if you want this other door to open. Many people feel that you can still be on dating sites or be dating around when God has told you that your person is not found there, but elsewhere. Disobedience blocks the blessing. You need to be focused and dedicate your time to praying for and preparing for the right person that God will bring you.

It Takes Time To Prep

It takes much time, energy and effort to prepare for a blessing to come. Remember that you are doing this in-and-around your regular workday and amid the myriad of chores and responsibilities you likely have. You need to make time in your day to visualize, to feel it, to prepare for it, to clear the space for it, and more. This is not done in five minutes and you need to make sure that you are doing everything you need to do to bring about your blessing. God has, is and will do His part - don't you worry about that. As long as you are praying, thanking and visualizing in faith, He is doing His part but you need to consistently do your part. How intensively you do it will also demonstrate how much you want it and how dedicated you will be to having it.

Take a few moments right now and think about how you will make time to prepare. Make a list of all the things you can think of that you will need to do to plan and prepare for this and then think about when you can make time to visualize its attainment. Be specific. Factor in all your other responsibilities and think realistically about when you will be able to dedicate yourself to doing this. Write it all down here and/or feel free to use your journal to jot this down:

12

Believing In You and Jesus Working Together

Psychologically, mentally, emotionally and spiritually, we must believe in ourselves and in God's ability to make things manifest in order for manifesting to occur. Yes, we need to believe in our own capabilities, that we are able to do this, that we will take or make the time to do this and to not doubt ourselves or God in His promises and in His abilities.

What do I mean by believing in yourself?

It means believing in what you are capable of doing through Christ. Believing in your abilities to manifest because you have taken the steps outlined. Believing in yourself and in your abilities does not mean that if it doesn't appear within a random time frame you have set for yourself, then it's not working. No. Instead, we have to accept that it will happen in God's timing and that just because it hasn't manifested when we wanted it to, that doesn't mean that it won't be manifesting at all.

Our Time Frame

Manifesting something does not happen in our time frame. I have to make this really clear because this is a common misconception that needs to be eradicated. It will likely not happen in your time frame but that doesn't mean it isn't happening. It is. It just will be at a different time than you might think. You see, God knows each of our situations intimately well. He knows how much you have in your bank account. He knows how much you want this or that. He knows all that is riding on all of these things. Remember, He is Omniscient (meaning He knows everything), and Omnipresent (meaning He is everywhere all at the same time). This means that He knows everything that you need and want and knows when and how to bring it to you. You may think you want A at X time but He knows that if you got A at that exact time of X, that it won't be a good idea for you for reasons that may not be immediately clear to you but if He doesn't bring it to you at X time, He is actually doing you a favor.

Taking the example of the Smiths (names changed). The Smiths were a lovely older couple who wanted to open up a bakery after they retired from their salaried jobs. Mrs. Smith was a wonderful baker (her friends and family had raved about her baked goods for years) and Mr. Smith was a whiz at accounting and numbers. They felt it made a perfect match and they were eager and excited to be doing something they both loved doing and promised themselves and each other they would set up a bakery after their retirement. They began scouting for locations and soon enough, they fell on two that could very well meet their needs. One was a larger location and the other a smaller one, both available at about the same time. They opted and wanted the smaller location, thinking that it would be enough for them and their customer's needs but the Smiths were praying people and they believed in and relied on God and His wisdom. They both prayed separately about it and they said that if it was God's will for them to have the smaller location, then He would make it happen. They went ahead and put in a lease offer. It was quickly rejected for reasons they did not receive. The owner would not rent to them and they were perplexed. Mr. Smith then remembered that they asked God not to let the deal happen if that was not His will, so they began praying and saying that if it was in fact His will for them to have the larger location, to please confirm that and to let that location fall into their laps. It fell into their laps almost instantly. Now, you may be thinking "Well how did God do them a favor by giving them a larger location with more expenses?" Well, what the Smiths didn't know is that God knew that covid was going to hit and that because of the added space and the location of the larger store, that they were able to open earlier than other retailers because they could allow for much more social distancing and on top of that, they ended up getting the larger location for just about the same amount as the smaller location. Plus, the larger location was very near in proximity to an office building, and much of the staff in all the offices were excited and keen to check out the baked goods Mrs. Smith would be offering. They are still doing very well today and enjoying the fruits of their faith in the Lord.

Another example of believing in yourself in manifestation is the example of Julia. Julia is a kind young woman who wanted to be married to the man God intended for her. She set aside time each day to visualize this in order to manifest and her family and friends were saying she was being foolish, that you don't meet men when you have your eyes closed, visualizing alone in your room. She persisted. She knew that visualizing daily would lead to the manifestation of her dreams and she knew that God was going to lead her to the right man. She spent hours visualizing a good, kind, solid, caring man who was also of faith and who would love her just as she is. A few months later, she felt compelled to join a soccer club and she met Paulo. Paulo was a good, kind, solid, caring man who was also of faith and....he adored Julia. He loved everything about her and was exactly what she had asked for. After a short courtship, he proposed and today, they are married with children (and she manifested the children as well, via the same means).

With these examples, I am showing you that when you do your part, believing in the process and relying on God's goodness, doing all that he calls you to do and working hard, He will do His part and He will cause it to manifest. The Smiths and Julia could easily have gotten tired, been annoyed, tried visualizing once or twice but thrown in the towel saying "This is stupid. It's not working. It's taking too long" but they didn't. They persisted and believed in God's promises and today, they are reaping the rewards.

When they say that the Word of God is like a seed planted, it really is. It is planted and then it takes work and time for it to grow and bear fruit. We can easily get annoyed and lose patience because we are not seeing the plant grow quickly enough, but we need to resolve for ourselves that we will remain steadfast in our faith and in the actions required to see the manifestation of the gifts of the planted seed. This is how faith works. This is how manifesting works.

13

The Way We Think

At first glance, one may not understand what this title means. It means that we think with our human minds, whereas God thinks with a Godly mind. In other words, He does not think the same way we do. This means that we have to rely on His thinking as much as possible because His way is ultimately the right way. To give you an example, if God says that He is going to "bless you", you could be thinking and interpreting it in one way but that is not necessarily the way He has intended it to be taken. You could be thinking He is going to bless you with much of this or that, but what He may have meant is that He is going to bless you by giving you a day full of sunshine. He can say that He is going to avenge you to people who have done you wrong but avenging you could mean many different things and it does not mean that He is going to avenge you today, or tomorrow or next week. Instead, He is going to do it in the timing that will reap the most benefit from the situation and in a way that will most benefit you and glorify Him. So the question then becomes: how do we know what He means?

Simple. We ask.

God loves being asked questions and He loves providing replies. He loves answering with long and detailed answers but we have to do our part and ask and probe and ask again and dive in deeper. That part is really important. Probe. Ask again. Inquire more deeply and thoroughly. And then get quiet and listen carefully because He will answer and He will tell you. In fact, Biblically, He longs for you to ask Him. He longs for us to come to Him with our questions, problems, concerns, wonderments, etc. And we need to be grateful that His personality is as such because it avails much to us in terms of blessings.

Here is some two-way journaling about this.

Me: Holy Spirit, what do You want to say about this?

H.S.: You're right. Everything you are writing here, you are right. People need to ask, ask, ask and probe, probe, probe. I always respond but they need to ask and inquire. Especially when people do not understand something, they don't ask. Many assume that I am just an unfair God who doesn't care about them. Nothing could be further from the truth. I want to bring them many blessings but if you don't check-in and activate the blessings, then people are not doing their part.

Me: Ok. Anything else?

H.S.: Definitely. Most people do not make time in their day to pray, much less visualize. The most successful people in the world are the ones who not only make this a regular practice but they also make sure to do this in intricate detail, to the point where they go dizzy seeing the details. That is active visualization and it's fantastic. If more people engaged in this in God's will, humanity would be at a very different space.

Me: Thank You, Holy Spirit.

H.S.: Anytime. Literally.

Why do we need to be grateful for this?

Imagine the alternative: imagine that we did not have the ability to hear from God and we did not have access to the wisest Mind in the world. Imagine that God did not wish to speak to us, to guide us and to show us what is real and what is not. God, in His infinite wisdom, knew that we would need Him and there is no shame in that. We were never supposed to "do" life on our own. We were always the sheep and He was always the Shepherd. The Shepherd provides for the sheep. When people go it on their own, they are making a choice to leave out the shepherd from their life and as such, are putting themselves squarely in danger. This is not wise.

"I don't know God yet"

This is a common explanation I hear from people who choose to go it on their own. Either they were never taught the Word of God, they had no exposure to Him or to His teachings, they were never given the tools to make the choice to follow Him but I will tell you, please use this book as your invitation to start that relationship today. Turning to Him and co-creating with Him is easy. Here is a suggested prayer you can pray (out loud or in your mind) where you can invite God into your life:

God, I don't know You and I never have but I desire an active, loving, vibrant and happy relationship with You. I repent of my sins and I desire to know You and to be led by You because You are God, You are wisdom, and You know best. I ask You to come into my life and to show me all that You want to show me. I ask You to come into my life and guide me as You need to. I ask You to show me how to have a loving, vibrant, active relationship with You. In Jesus' name. Amen

This is a powerful, inviting prayer, asking God to come into your life and as He too wants a relationship with you, He will answer you.

The Bible's Relevance

Some people say or think the Bible is just an old book, with no relevance to life today. That is not true. The Bible is not only relevant to today's life but it is timeless - meaning that its teachings are valid for all of time. The Bible's concepts and teachings cover every aspect of life so we can be wise and understand the way the world works.

In other words, the Bible is the inerrant Word of God and within its pages, it explains to us who God is, what He wills for us, what He and we are capable of and much more.

Human Nature & God's Provision

The Bible is a timeless book. A timeless treasure, really. It explains fundamental truths, concepts and reality. It talks about true human nature and dives in deeply to demonstrate the personality of God and how He operates. It also goes to show how God consistently did and does provide for us throughout history and today. He has provided for us in all of the following ways:

- Given us earth and all that exists on it
- Given us food, health, nutrition
- A sound mind
- A sound body
- Languages
- Laughter
- Making love
- Having family & descendants
- Money and how to increase the resource in our lives

- How to be proper stewards of all our resources
- Friends and companionship
- Marriage
- Jesus
- The Holy Spirit and as such, a moral compass that is housed within our very bodies
- Minds and reasoning to think, deduce and make good choices
- Cattle and food of all kinds
- Trees
- The sun
- Visualization
- Manifestation
- Learning obedience
- Relationship with Him

I can go on but I think you get the point. He has always provided for us and will continue to do so but many don't pay attention to Him, don't ask Him questions, they don't know His ways and they assume that He does not operate today.

This is why I have decided to include this section into this book. We have been given, among many other things, the benefits of visualization as a means to manifest, so we can literally go to Him and ask Him to bring any good thing that we desire.

Erroneous Human Thinking

In my conversation one time with a woman I will name Joyce, I had mentioned that I am writing a book about manifesting and another about God and Prosperity. I mentioned that I am looking to show and explain to people that God does want us to be prosperous in all ways: in health, in wealth, in sound mind, body and soul, etc. Her comment was "Oh you think so, huh?!" My answers then and now are still the same.

Of course God wants us to be very successful and prosperous. Why would she think God does not want us to be prosperous? Successful? Have all the good things that life has to offer? Let's look at the Biblical evidence of this:

- Jesus looked for fishers of men to bring the good news about all that is available to those who believed
- Jesus provided wine (merry-making) as His first miracle
- Jesus provided food for the gatherers when all the disciples had with them was a few loaves of bread and some fish
- Jesus provided healing for the sick and the demon-possessed
- Jesus provided His life as a sacrifice to those who believe in Him
- Jesus provided an example of love and acceptance when He implored everyone to throw the first rock on their woman who had sinned if any of them were free of sin
- Jesus provided comfort for those who witnessed or heard of the miracles He had been doing because if He could heal those people, it gave hope that He could heal all people
- Jesus provided an example for how to deal with the enemy in a strategic way
- He provided some money to the men whom He advised to invest the money and not just bury it

As you can see, God has provided for us not only for mind and body and soul but also for our finances. He wants us to wisely invest our money and to see it grow. He also provides returns when we engage in the ancient custom of tithing (the giving of the first 10% of your income) to organizations that are dedicated to Him, such as Christ-centered soup kitchens, charities that honor Him, Christian health centers, Bible-based Churches and more. You will know that an organization is dedicated to Him because they put Him, His concepts and His teachings front and center.

14

How To Keep In Faith While Waiting

It can be tough to stay in faith while we are waiting for something to manifest. The question then becomes: what do we do while we wait? All of the following apply:

- Keep thanking God for bringing it
- Keep busy and try to keep your mind off of it
- Spend time being of service to others
- Read the Bible for inspiration
- Read the promises He gave to you that He will bring your blessing to come to pass
- Read testimonials of others who have experienced their miracle
- Work and do things God has already brought you
- Continue visualizing even as you go through your day
- Stay in faith, however you need to do that (some people find it helpful to put a cross in their car, to put posters and wooden quote plaques around their home or office, some others yet enjoy listening to and singing songs of worship and praise, etc.)

One way that I try to stay in faith while waiting for my manifested blessing is to watch the clouds moving. I didn't ask them to move and yet there they are, moving along. This is a bit of an indication to me that God is doing, working and arranging things. It's my comforting indicator that He is moving things in my favor "up there".

The Wisdom of Songs of Praise and Worship

God enjoys being worshiped. He enjoys knowing and seeing that we are demonstrating faith in Him and worshiping who He is. He enjoys knowing that you are using His Word to further your life in the ways that He calls you to do so. Another thing God loves is when people sing songs of praise and worship to Him - He enjoys this because it tells Him that you know that He is God and that you are relying on Him. People often enjoy being needed. God is no different. When you are praying, post-praying and waiting, God loves being sung to and enjoys receiving words of praise. He loves knowing that you are giving Him the glory and that you are thanking Him for being Who He is and know that He is working on your behalf.

There are many wonderful bands and individual singers who have such anointings that they create the most wonderful, God-inspired music. They sing songs that demonstrate how awesome He is, how much good He has done in their lives, and how the singers have faith that He will do more wonderful works in their lives. It is really astounding to read the worship lyrics from different bands and to hear their touching musical notes, beats and sounds.

Even listening to music or singing songs of worship in your car as you are driving, as you are going about your day or your errands, doing your home chores, etc., will all serve to uplift you and to remember God's goodness. These will go a long way in helping to manifest your blessings.

Doing Nothing vs. Waiting

I remember when I was starting my walk with God, I remember this teaching. With the benefit of a few more years behind me and a more "mature" (let's call it that) perspective, I can reflect on this and know that it is so very true. There is a very big difference between doing nothing and waiting on God after we have prayed for something. Doing nothing means not furthering your goals, not advancing what God has put on your heart and not working toward it. Waiting on God means you have prayed, you have and you are doing everything action-wise that you have needed to do and now, you are just waiting on Him.

God works and operates in ways that we do not and cannot understand. He works at all times and according to Scripture, never stops working. This means that when you have done all you can, He is going to do for you what you couldn't make happen on your own. One of the best examples of this is when a man I heard about was getting ready to put in his mortgage application. He was on a very tight income and was hoping and praying for a low interest rate from the bank, at a time when interest rates were extremely high. He put in his mortgage application, completed all the required documents and was now just waiting for the mortgage loan to be approved. He didn't have the best financial and credit history and the loan interest rate that he had applied for was very low. If he didn't get this loan, he would not have been able to afford the house, very simply and he prayed that if the acquisition of this house was the Lord's will, that he would be approved for the loan. He waited one day, two days, three days worrying that he was not going to get it. The day before the house was supposed to close, he got the approval that he needed. He was able to buy the house and he would have been able to afford the loan.

The lesson here is that we need to do our best and take strategic, inspired action as we are guided, and let God do what He needs to do that we cannot make happen on our own.

15

It Manifested! Now What??

When the manifestation happens, we have now received what we asked for. Again, it may not look exactly as you thought it would, but it has manifested. Now that it has, what do we do?

Well, first, we thank God for providing and we are joyful about what has just happened. Next, we want to remain in thanks and maybe even write out how God came through for us in the form of a testimonial. Why a testimonial? Because when others know and hear about how God worked in your life, they too will feel more confident and encouraged to come to God and to ask Him to bless them with things that are in His will. People need to see that God is definitely still in the business of doing miracles and it would benefit people tremendously if they see what you did and how you leaned on Him to produce miracles in your life so that He will also work in theirs. Also, keep in mind that now that you have experienced this miracle, you have a better sense of how God actually works, so you know what to look for next time, what to do, how to be and stay in gratitude, etc.

I think I would be hard-pressed to find someone who isn't happy and grateful when their miracle manifests, so enjoy the moment when it happens. Dance in your home or in your car, get on your knees and say thank You again to God, celebrate and enjoy the moment and the blessing because it is the result of yours and God's hard work.

I have seen some people not be happy when their miracle manifested, for one reason or another, and I don't understand that. Some might say it didn't look anything like what they thought it would or it doesn't feel like they thought it would. I urge people who say that or think that to reconsider. They have received a wonderful blessing from God and the response really should be of happy gratitude. God will not be inclined to bring more goodness to those who are not thankful for what He has already given them.

Protecting Your Blessing

A blessing does need to be protected. Some people will want to take your blessings away from you out of spite, jealousy, etc. We need to protect what we have worked so hard to get. How do we do that? We ask the same God who brought us the blessing to protect it for us.

We do this by praying regularly for our blessings to be sheltered, and protected. I will give you an example here of a blessing that became threatened: Jana and Mark were a married couple whose union was blessed by God. God brought them together, blessed them with children and with a happy marriage and showered them with an unsurpassed love for each other. After some time, Mark fell into alcoholism and Jana fell into a pornography addiction. These were both beginning to take their toll on their marriage and because of the shame they felt for being addicted, they began to hide their feelings and their addictions from each other. This separation began slowly at first but then when it became compounded by the fact that their kids were starting to fail in school, everything blew up. They began yelling at each other, they began withholding their thoughts and their feelings, they began to accuse each other of unpleasant things, and the list goes on. When I met them, they were at the height of their "blame game" as some called it. It took months of counseling, therapy and opening up honestly and openly with each other for them to realize that these things were destroying their marriage. They began to pray over their marriage and for the strength to get back to a good and happy place where they once were.

We need to remember to consistently give thanks and to pray for protection over our blessings so that we can continue to enjoy the fruits of what God has given us.

What Do I Have To Be Thankful For?

I have heard many people ask this question. Some may be down on their luck and feel there isn't much to be thankful for. There are always things to be thankful for and keep in mind that many of these blessings are things you may not even ever have asked for - they are just blessings that God has given you from the goodness of His heart:

- Your breath
- The ability to smile
- The ability to walk
- The gift of vision
- The ability to love
- The sunshine
- A good night's sleep
- Friends
- Family
- Loved ones
- The joy you get from hobbies and things you love to do

I understand that some people reading this may not feel great about their lives all the time and their circumstances may make it challenging to feel gratitude but we all have reasons to be grateful for something. If you think your blessing is so insignificant, look to someone who doesn't have what you have.

Sometimes, people will take the one thing they don't have yet and they will use that as a reason to be unhappy. I was talking with a man one time who said he was depressed. He had a beautiful house he owned, was doing very well in his career, was handsome by all accounts and had many friends. Because he was not yet married and he desired to be so, he considered his life unhappy and he went around with that unhappy "cloud" hanging over his head each and every single day. There were many things he could have done to help himself with his "singledom" but the fact that he couldn't consider himself blessed at all because this one thing was missing from his life is the part that I don't believe is wise.

God helps those who help themselves. I'm going to say that again to help make sure it really sinks in: God helps those who help themselves. One more time for effect: God helps those who help themselves.

Ask Him how He wants you to proceed in attaining the desires He has put on your heart and He will tell you. Then, do those things in the measure & in the timing He guides, leaving the ultimate attainment of it to Him and His timing.

You Do Not Make It Happen...He Does

Some people erroneously believe that they should be making things happen in their own strength, like Abraham did in the Bible. This is especially for people who have been waiting a while (or a long time) and have not yet seen their blessing manifest. Biblically, this was the case of Abraham, who felt he had waited long enough and wanted to make the heir promised to him happen right away. He was not willing to wait anymore on God's timing so he just worked (works of the flesh) to make it happen. It happened, alright, but the son produced by the works of the flesh was not the promised son. This is what God told Abraham as well and it resulted in difficulties ensuing as a result.

Don't try to make it happen on your own time frame. As humans, that is not something we love to hear (I know I didn't enjoy hearing it when I did) but we have to accept it. When we accept co-creating with God, we have to accept the time frame and the ways in which He gives it.

Give It To God

This is such an important concept.

When we give something to God, we are saying: "God, take this problem out of my hands - I am taking my hands off the wheel, and giving this problem to You, God, because I am unable to handle it. This problem is too big for me and You know what to do with it in a way that I do not and cannot." Then, you take your hands off the wheel and you stop worrying about it.

He Is Qualified

God caused worlds to come into place with just the power of His spoken words. As such, I think it's safe to say that He can handle all of your problems, my problems, and everyone else on earth's problems and then some.

As such, when we practice visualization and manifestation, we are in effect giving the problem to God because He is the One who is going to cause the manifestation to happen. He is the One who is going to cause things to happen that you could not make happen on your own. So when I say give it to God, that is what I mean. In my illustrated book with the same title (Give it to God), I again present this concept of giving it to God with simple illustrations, reminding the reader that letting Him do what He needs to do in the time frame that He needs to do it in is what you are asking for and accepting. This means that we have to sit back and wait in faith while He works to bring it to us, only taking inspired action when He tells us to.

Examples:

1. Gerry wanted to meet his future wife and get on with his life. I prayed and suggested he pray about this and then leave it to God. God presented him with a woman through a real estate agent he had worked with only once before. Today, they are married with their first child on the way.
2. Joe wanted to marry his best friend but didn't know how. He prayed for it and began prepping for it, just like I advised him to do after I had prayed about it and sure enough, several months later, they got engaged and they had their third just a short while ago.
3. Vivian wanted her family's investment property rented out. It was taking a very long time and the area and plot restrictions seemed to be suffocating any possibilities. The lease was not forthcoming. I prayed about it and I advised her to stop complaining about it (yes, complaining most definitely hinders the process - more on that later) and to leave it with God. Within 4 months, they had a wonderful lease offer for a 5-year term that would benefit them tremendously and cause much prosperity.
4. Ger had a cardiac episode and passed out. His family (who was attending a funeral that day and were all on their way into the service) found him passed out, looking white-as-a-sheet, on the parking lot floor, blood seeping from his head. A nearby doctor pounded on his chest (they didn't have a defibrillator with them)

for several minutes, his sister holding his tongue with a tissue so that he doesn't choke on his tongue. His niece privately prayed to God and asked Him not to take her uncle (who had not yet repented) and gave the problem to God. The ambulance was taking forever to get there, even though this had happened on the grounds of a hospital. He was finally taken by ambulance and the other family members went into the funeral service. A little over two hours later, they received word that Ger was fine and not only that, that the chances of him having gotten out of that ordeal without any brain damage was less than 2%. He was that lucky.

5. Suzy wanted to be married to a man of the same ethnic background. She didn't go out much so she didn't know where she was going to meet him. She decided to listen to me and to pray for God to bring her the right man. A year later, she married Aram, a man she was crazy about and who was of the same ethnic background.

6. Caroline wanted to publish her books and so after she wrote the manuscripts, she decided she would send in the necessary documentation to various prospective publishers, and then she decided to give it to God. He guided her to be obedient about something unrelated, even though she did not want to be obedient about that matter. She chose to be obedient about it and the very next day, she received an offer to publish in her email inbox, offering to publish her very first book.

7. Diana and Rock wanted to have their first child but Diana had discovered that she was unable to carry children. After going to Church to get wisdom about the situation, the Pastor wisely suggested they pray about it and then give it to God. Not a month later, Diana's sister selflessly offered to be her surrogate at no charge and to carry their baby for them. Today, Diana and Rock are the proud parents of happy and healthy twins.

8. Gary was in the process of having a stroke. His family did not know that this was happening so they didn't get alarmed until it

became apparent later on. As the stroke's effects were taking their toll on him, his family decided he should go to the emergency room. He agreed but it was difficult getting him there because at that point, he was having trouble with something as simple as putting on his shoes. As they were going to the emergency room, his family prayed and they gave the situation to God. Three hours later, his family had gotten word that he needed a shot to stop the brain's bleeding and that he would be fine, The doctors advised that he may not be the exact same after the effects but the family held faith that he would be near-normal because they gave the problem to God, who can do literally anything. Sure enough, today, Gary is ok and the after-effects of the stroke are not anywhere near what they could have been, not to mention that his family and friends still get to have him around and enjoy him.

Friends, I can give you many more examples of how God comes through but I think you are getting the point.

16

Where You Start Doesn't Matter. Just Start.

This is a very important point. It doesn't really matter where you start. Just start and you will see things moving, shifting, changing in the right direction. Simply put: visualizing and manifesting works for everyone who works at them and dedicates themselves to their practices. You don't have to be from the right family, you don't have to have gone to a certain school or have started working at a certain age or have this professional connection or that one.

Fact is: God overrules all of it and when He says He is going to bless you with it, you can take that as a promise that He will fulfill. The only catch is: you have to keep doing your part based on the process outlined. That sounds like a pretty good deal to me, don't you think?!

It's such a wonderful and liberating feeling to know that you don't have to have been from a certain background, from a certain geographic location, have a certain connection...nope....God overrules all of that and He will be the One to bring the blessing to you.

I will not forget how I was dealing with a legal case with a particularly nasty fellow who did not want to do the right thing and make his contractual payments. I was in way over my head and I had no idea how I was going to afford to maintain my own finances, let alone pay for the legal fees that I figured were inevitably going to be part of this. To say the least: the situation sucked. God put it on my heart that it was He (not any lawyer or legal system) that was going to vindicate me. Upon being guided to do so, I spent some time dealing with the legal system, only to see how it was not working in any way and I was getting nowhere fast, all with the legal fees piling up. Then, the Lord made it clear that I was going to find my vindication and solace in Him with this situation, not in the legal system. So, I wait for the manifestation of my promise.

God Overrules

The fact is: God overrules all. If there is a promise He has made to you, a dream He has given you, a desired possibility that will present itself, then He will do what needs to be done in the situation. All the lawyers in the world and all the officials can say what they want - when God says it's done, it is done.

Many reading this may say "But Christine, it hasn't happened yet, and I don't know when it will". Yes, this is where faith comes in. This is where we have to let God do what He needs to do and we have to be patient. The example of Roberta comes to mind here.

Roberta is a lady going through a very contentious divorce and custody battle. Her husband had been philandering for years, and left her with a crushing debt, and she had to sell the house to pay for that debt. In the blink of an eye, she went from a married homeowner to a divorced renter who was barely able to make ends meet. To make matters worse, her estranged husband had been having an affair and was an alcoholic who had hit one of their children on one occasion. The problems she was facing were too much for her, so I advised her to give the problem to God and to proceed with her life as best as she could.

Nobody is too far gone to give the problem to God and there is no bad or wrong time to give Him the problem. Yes, the sooner you give it the better but you can give it to Him at any time.

Money Is Never A Barrier to God's Goodness

Many reading this may say: "Christine, I don't come from a wealthy family who is able to do this and do that, with lots of connections" or "How am I going to get this when I clearly don't have the money to do so?" or "I don't have the money to get out of this legal situation". When you give it to God, He knows exactly what He's doing, exactly what's in your bank account, exactly how much things cost and He gave you the dream anyway. He wouldn't bring it if He didn't have a way to bring it to come to pass. He is going to make it happen in His way and in His timing in a way you may not have been able to see coming. I have seen this happen again and again in peoples' lives all around me and with people from all over the world, including in my own life so I know that He fulfills His promises.

Not Limited to Money

I'd like to point out that His promises don't just have to do with money or position. I have seen Him allow babies to be conceived and delivered, happy and healthy, to the most joyful and grateful parents and guardians, whom people and doctors assumed would never get to be parents and to love and raise a child. Women who were "too old" or who had a womb that doctors said would not safely carry a baby were the very ones God blessed and showed them that their desire to be a parent would be fulfilled.

I saw as God transformed the situation of people who could not read and could not write become scholars and PhDs. I watched as God gave sight to people otherwise blind and how He blessed them with amazing vision.

In sum, no matter where you are, how old you are, what your background is...it doesn't matter. If you invite the Lord into your life, He will be there and He will love you and help you exactly where you are and with whatever you have to get started with. Then, a fantastic transformation takes place and He helps you realize things you may not have paid attention to in the past.

So, while I make the point of getting your walk started with the help of such Preachers, there is also no substitute for actually reading the Word of God and praying to the Holy Spirit to help you understand what you are reading and the messages in both the text and the subtext. That prayer can be as simple as

Holy Spirit, I thank You for having brought me this reading material. I pray for You to help me understand all that I am reading and I pray for You to help me to really apply the concepts of what I am reading to my life. Please give me visuals and help me to really understand how this material may apply to my own life. In Jesus' name. Amen.

17

Do I Have To Already Have a Relationship with God?

You do not. But you will want to have a relationship with God because it will be the beginning of a renewed mind, superior understanding, wisdom, strategy, unconditional love, unsurpassed wealth, great forgiveness, and best of all, salvation. God longs to be in your life in a way that you may not currently understand.

I used to be totally confused when people said that they had a walk with God. I was like "You're walking with God? How?" It is only later that I learned that because we say that life is a journey that we say that we are walking with Him. In reality, we are walking with Him, running with Him, sitting with Him, contemplating with Him, praying and visualizing with Him, crying with Him, talking and sharing with Him, relying on Him, responding to Him, and so much more. We are allowing ourselves to engage with an invisible Spirit but One that we can sense and feel clearly when we take the time to still ourselves and to hear from Him clearly. It is often best to shut out the noise of the world in order to hear from Him correctly and without interference.

Many have asked me "Is it just like the waves of a radio station? Is that what you mean by the frequency and hearing clearly?" And I reply "Yes, it is like that but it is also like listening to your best friend talking to you in a very crowded area and so you sometimes want to get to an area where there is no noise so you can hear your best friend more clearly."

So, you don't have to already have a relationship with God in order to hear Him correctly but He is inviting you into a relationship with Him where He wants you to:

- Talk to Him
- Laugh with Him
- Cry with Him
- Share your joys with Him
- Share your worries with Him
- Unload on Him
- Pray to Him
- Rely on Him
- Lean on Him
- Ask Him for help with everything
- Give it to Him (and by it, I mean problems)
- Ask Him for wisdom and insight

As you can see, He wants you to go to Him with everything because He desires to be in every area of your life today, tomorrow and every day, even if you have never gone to Him before. One of the most interesting things is that whether we are in relationship with Him or not, He already knows everything about us and loves everything about us.

I have heard others many times say that the Lord told me this or that about myself, things I didn't even know about myself. My response is always "Well, of course, He knows you the best because He created you." As I say in my first illustrated book "Jesus Loves You", He is the One who knit you together in your mother's womb and so He knew you before you were even born. He knew you before the formation of the world. He knew all you would do, all you would think, all you would become even before you were born.

My intent in telling you this is so that you will know that you have a kind and loving Father who is there for you and loves you unconditionally, not to scare you or worry you. Some people reading this may think or feel that they are too far gone, too far gone in the wrong direction for God to love them, care for them or want a relationship with you. Far from it! Despite what you may have done, the wrongs you may have committed, etc., He still loves you and still wants to help you through relationship with you.

Will you let Him in?

What Complaining Does

Simply put: complaining does the exact opposite of what you want it to do, it stops the blessing from coming. Complaining about a problem or a situation you have asked Him to help you with and/or that you are visualizing about will literally stop the blessing from coming. Again, I will explain my own experience below of how I know this:

My Own Experience

A family member of mine owned a beautiful property. They had purchased it as an investment property with the obvious goal being to make money from it. Due to zoning issues and bylaws, they were not able to rent it out for many years (yes, I said years, not months). Everyone in the family started to complain about everything about the situation. The complaining was not just once or twice but a manifestation of our collective frustration at the situation and how we all felt so hopeless about the situation. We were (with our own human and limited lens) looking at possible solutions but nothing had been working for a long time. The costs were mounting and were phenomenal, the situation was getting worse and worse and there was literally nobody who could (or was) helping.

A good Christian friend suggested I give the problem to God. Whether it was out of frustration or desperation, I chose to give the problem to God. I could sense in my spirit that things were shifting and something was happening but there was no official word yet and so I had no concrete evidence of anything happening or improving.

The family's complaining didn't stop.

At one point, I felt God was trying to tell me something so I went for a long drive to blow off some steam and to gain some perspective. God made it so clear to me that I needed to stop my own complaining and the family needed to stop complaining. I understood. The complaining was blocking the blessing. I went home and asked everyone to stop complaining because I was actively praying for a solution. The complaining halted. Soon thereafter, the solution came: we were presented with a lease offer that was not only fair and acceptable, but that responded to and complied with all the area and building bylaws. It was literally an answer from God! Today, that property is still rented and my family member still enjoys the fruits of that. Now, I have to note here that we also need to ask God to protect the blessings that He has brought us, because the darkness likes to attack and try to steal away the good that the Lord has brought us.

So, the lesson here: complaining stops the blessing from manifesting, even when you visualize, so please stop if you want to see the manifestation happen.

Gratitude and thanking God in the midst of the difficulties actually encourages Him and propels Him to do more for us and to act more swiftly on our behalf. So, you know what to do! :) Why is this so? Because God has already given us much. He has already given us so much and His nature is that He is prompted to provide more when we are thankful for what He has already provided. Complaining is essentially you telling Him that you are not grateful so why would He give you more?

18

Powerful Acts

The fact is, visualizing, praying and manifesting are powerful acts. Even putting up pictures on a vision board is a powerful act. By simply keeping these visionary goals in front of you, you are essentially re-focusing your attention and re-focusing your mind's power over to these things. With each new viewing, your brain is essentially beginning to compute how we can achieve these things, what steps and assumptions and plans are required. It really is quite an amazing process.

I recall that when I had on my vision board that I wanted to write a certain number of books each year (which was a very ambitious number for any person), and I began to mentally compute how I can arrange my time, my schedule, my day and my actions to the realization and completion of that. Said differently, I began to think about how I can become a lean, mean writing machine and put out books that were super informative, engaging, real and true-to-life circumstances, and that would thoroughly explain what I needed to get across to my readers. I began paying attention to the strategies used by prolific authors (much more prolific than I) and how to write books that called the reader, even beckoned to them to pick up this book because it was written so well and was so effective in its approach and in its explanations that people couldn't help but to buy them. I essentially began to devise a way to make it happen.

Putting up pictures and engaging in these acts also takes a fair bit of chutzpah and belief in oneself. The accomplishment of any goal does. You need to dedicate yourself to it, overcome the challenges and the hurdles, sacrifice other things and other actions and much more.

Take the example of a person who is looking to lose weight and has included that in their prayers and on their vision board. They need to mentally get in the frame of mind of all of the following: they need to count calories and (now) be very mentally conscious of what they consume, they need to work out and have the necessary facilities to do those workouts and to spend money to buy workout clothes and they need to ensure that they are replenishing their bodies with the needed proteins and water intake, they need to refrain (or at least seriously reduce) their sugar and fat intake (which will now change and affect the way they grocery shop), they will need to stay away from white breads and pastas (again, a possible shift in their grocery list and their taste palate because whole wheat pasta tastes different from white pastas and rice), and they will be doing this not over days or weeks but over months and years. It takes a complete shift in your thinking and in your attitudes. I will definitely argue that losing weight is an emotional journey because I myself went through many different emotions as one who was trying to lose weight. When I saw a picture of myself from past days, I went into a shock. I had never seen myself as an overweight woman but there it was: many many extra pounds hanging on me and over me. It was a very difficult beginning for me because I had to cut out all the foods and desserts that contribute to making us that way (cakes, cookies, white breads, sweets, sugar, high-fat foods) and I had to stop myself from all of that. I even remember the day my naturopath said to me that I needed to look carefully at everything I was eating and carefully consider all items. I began to realize that sometimes, my latte was way too sweet and that the Chinese food takeout I was getting was (part of it) deep fried (I didn't know that) and that when I asked them to make it with water and not with oil, the taste would be totally different but I chose that it was worth it.

My goal was to become fit and very lean and that was going to mean that I wouldn't be able to consume the same things in the same way. It is a price to pay for looking and being different. I found that in order to accomplish great things, we sometimes need to do things that others might think are a little bit "out there". My whole family thinks that the super lean birthday cakes I request for my celebration are a little "out there" but that's ok. That's how I need to eat to achieve and maintain the physique I desire and that I feel called to have.

When you make choices to follow-through on the dreams and goals that God is calling you to undertake, nobody promised it would be easy and nobody promised that you would be able to do it without criticism. We have to do it despite and in the face of criticism. God is our strength and our salvation - when you need strength and you need to lean on someone, lean on Him. He wants to be there to help you through it all and He is looking to be a wonderful partner in all these things with you.

> **We have to do it despite and in the face of criticism.**

People Being Against You

In a book about visualizing and manifesting, I also need to touch on this point. Simply put: not everyone is going to be "for" you. Not everyone is going to support you. Not everyone wants to be your ally and some will be outright against you and will work against you. Jesus also had tremendous opposition but He persevered and He turned to Father God to help him through all of it and He succeeded in His goals.

You have the same power on your side. Put differently, God is with you too and He expected the opposition, He knew it would be coming, He knew who, when, where and how, and also why. Everyone has a why for their actions. The reasons behind what they do. And their why might surprise you but nonetheless, it is there and when it comes, we need to rely on God to help get us through it. Jesus also relied on God and God helped him. He was there for Him, supported Him, loved Him and more.

The good news, though, is that God won't allow these challenges to persist forever. He will allow them for a time but then they will pass and through them, He will protect you and He will help you. You will go through the proverbial fire but as you are going through that, it is really important to remember that what He brought you to, He will see you through. He will deliver you from it and He will help you through it.

I remember one lady I was speaking to who was telling me about some health difficulties she had been experiencing. She was saying how totally difficult it was to be going through those things and how difficult it was because in the meantime, her husband of many years also told her he was going to be leaving here because he had met someone else. She was devastated and going through the proverbial fire! She knew that she needed to lean on and rely heavily on God's goodness through the difficulties and that she would need to have a certain positive mindset to get through everything. Ultimately, she decided to begin by creating a vision board full of all the happy things she felt inspired to ask the Lord to bring into her life: total health, a dedicated and loving husband, loving healthy and happy children, a new career that would make her much more money and provide her with benefits so that she could continue taking the necessary medications and have those health benefits, and she also wanted a dog. She put all these things on her vision board and she spent time each day seeing her goals in her mind, feeling the happiness despite all that was actually going on around her and she began to see her life changing in her mind. She replaced feelings of worthlessness and anxiety about her husband leaving with feelings of God's love for her as His daughter and she reminded herself of the Biblical words "I have give you a sound mind and body" which means that when she remembers those words, she remembers God's promise that He will give her back her health. She spent time each day thinking of and remembering all of God's good promises in her life and how she wanted to live each day thanking Him in advance for the new (better) life He was bringing her.

Slowly, things started shifting in that direction. The divorce became final and she ended up meeting a new companion who was a dedicated gardener like her and with whom she spent hours talking about their mutual love for all that they were growing, this man had a son whom she adored and got along with very well but the Lord also (while delivering her from the sickness) had also found means to get her pregnant after she married this fellow dedicated gardener. Another thing that tickled her was the fact that she had been offered her dream job at a home and garden magazine, where she could share with readers her wonderful tips for improving your garden and how to grow things organically.

You see, the Lord completely changed her life for the better because she used these tools, had faith in the Lord and His promises and she dedicated herself to the accomplishment of these things.

Another example is that of Becca. Becca is a kind and sensitive young lady who was full of life but because of her size, she had been mocked throughout life for being "too big" and as a result of her low self-esteem, she hadn't strived for much in life. She felt she didn't deserve much and her dad's criticisms of her body and her appearance had taken their toll on her her entire life. She didn't think she deserved better and so she didn't strive or try for better. As such, she had a career that really wasn't challenging her in any meaningful way, she married the first man who would take her and she didn't follow through on the singing career she had wanted since she was a little girl. I advised her to do the same things I am telling you to do in this book. Very slowly, she began putting these things in place and slowly, the tide for her started to turn. She had a conversation with her dad where she advised him that if he continued to put her down, that he would no longer have a relationship with her, she talked to her husband about their marriage and because his feelings for her were not deep, their marriage imploded. She decided to "get back out there" and to pray for a man who really loved her and today, she is doing as God led, she is on dating websites and has opened herself to meeting the man of her dreams and finally, she left her dead-end job and chose to pursue her God-given dream of owning a little bakery. She bakes each day and while she controls her own intake, she loves the joy she sees on the faces of her clients who buy her cakes for theirs or a family member's birthday and for their special occasions, and best of all, she now goes to Church regularly and enjoys learning about how God loves her unconditionally, despite not having a dad who treated her the way she was supposed to be treated. Becca's life was completely changed.

You see, dear reader, God knows exactly what you need and when you need it. He knows how to bring you every good and meaningful thing and He loves to bless His children with these things. He enjoys giving us things that are right for us and no, there is no need to scheme to get those things or to take something away from another because He has a great plan for every single one of our lives. More on this in the section below.

He Has A Great Plan For Each Of Us

God has a great plan for each one of us. He has a plan that will honor your talents. Some people think that in order to accomplish something, they need to be in competition with others. Not so. He has devised a plan for every person's life and while you do need to work hard and break down doors called challenges, you don't need to steal and to take from others. God has provided more than enough and when you follow His ways that He tells you to take, you will find that provision is there.

I also want to tell you that the plan for your life will be different from someone else's, so if you see that things are going differently for you than they are for someone else, take heart and know that this is not because God has something against you or is trying to make life more difficult. It just means that for one reason or another, your set of circumstances will be different.

Take the example of Nick Vujicic, the Australian Evangelist. Nick is an Evangelist and he preaches the Word of God but his path and his circumstances are very different than, say, another Evangelist's. In short, Nick was born without arms and legs. He does not have the use of these ligaments at his disposal and as you can imagine, this makes life very different for him. He cannot minister in the exact same way as others, he cannot preach while pacing back-and-forth on a stage like other Evangelists. He still does his work but in a different, and no less meaningful of a way. In fact, I would dare argue that even though Nick has this additional challenge in front of him, that his sermons and the creative ways he delivers them serve as a wonderful reminder to people who are going through their own challenges that they need to persevere, to keep going and to ask God for His help through it all.

Here is a lovely visual I came across that I think is perfect for the illustrations I am making in this section:

Nick Vujicic and Bethany Hamilton are two people who have some definite physical challenges they are dealing with but as you can see from this picture, they are still enjoying life, they are still taking part in fun (and a bit risky) activities, they are still smiling and enjoying a good life and they are doing it all in the face of some difficult circumstances that maybe some others of us don't have to deal with.

This picture is a good reminder that we need to take inventory of the blessings we may have taken for granted, such as being able to walk, having all your limbs, and the attitude that you can and will enjoy and appreciate all that life has to offer you, despite whatever challenges you are dealing with today or tomorrow.

Taking it one step further, it is a lot of how you choose to see things. To illustrate, Nick and Bethany could have been mad at God and decided to turn their backs to him. They could have decided that they would be mad at the world and not be positive or productive in any way. They could have decided that they do not want to see any positives and they could have taken drastic negative action, as many other people have done. Instead, they chose and choose to lean into who God is and to not only see the positive and deeper meaning behind their circumstances but they also choose to show others how to be positive. **They are inspiring others in the face of their own difficulties. That is inspirational and amazing.**

 I want to pause here for a moment and give you an opportunity to take another look at the blessings you have in your life. Take a look at the list you already made from the previous exercise and if you can think of more things, add to your list. If you wish to include these in your journal or in your phone or whatever device you use, do so because it should be included in a place where you know you will see it again and again.

Go right ahead and add more of your blessings in the space provided. Remember also that being positive and being an inspiration to others (you may not even know how you have inspired others) should also be noted here. Think of times where someone may have told you how great you are, how much you helped them, that you put a smile on their face, maybe a time when your child looked adoringly at you and much more.

MANIFEST IT! - 137

19

Seeing And Focusing On The Fine Details

Two things that make visualization to manifest so effective are:

1. to see the fine, intricate details of the image.
2. to not allow yourself to be interrupted.

Example 1:
Regarding step 1, for a person who has received a less-than-desired medical report, they can begin by looking at a medical report, we can see the doctor's notes on the chart. When you believe and are visualizing healing, you can start by seeing your version of the medical report (unless you are in the medical profession, you are not likely to know what the report actually looks like and you don't need to). You can re-write the medical report in your mind and have it read what you want it to read. You can see the fine details of some key and choice words in ink on the page writing "in complete health" and "no health issues remain". Spend time in your mind's eye visualizing key words like that and when you see those words written in your mind and your imagination, stay

focused on them, letting them stay on your mind, feeling the joyful feelings and letting the peace of the new diagnosis absorb into your whole being. Regarding step 2, while you are visualizing, do your best to not allow yourself to have interruptions. Even a phone vibrating can be an interruption that can pull away your attention and your focus from what you are seeing in very intricate detail.

Example 2:
Regarding step 1, for a person who would like to get engaged to be married, they can begin by seeing the diamond engagement ring and their wedding ring on *that* finger, feeling the rings between their fingers, playing with them and carefully feeling the ridges of the rings on their finger. They can see others congratulating them on their engagement and their marriage and they can imagine seeing the intricate details of their signed and certified marriage certificate in their possession. Regarding step 2, while you are visualizing, do your best to not allow yourself to have interruptions. Even a phone vibrating can be an interruption that can pull away your attention and your focus from what you are seeing and working on.

Example 3:
Regarding step 1, a person who has an addiction of any kind can see themselves as fully healed, can imagine the intricate details of their bodies no longer craving that thing that isn't good for them and can see the intricate details of no longer be attached to the addiction but instead, going about their lives easily and without that anchor. They can really deep-dive into the feelings of feeling great and being free from that addiction. Regarding step 2, they need to make sure that they have no interruptions around them while they are doing this. Having interruptions will break concentration and will not allow for a sustained envisioning of their goals and will break the good and positive feelings associated.

Example 4:

Regarding step 1, a person who is envisioning a job or career change can see an email they have received offering them the new employment, the benefits they will be receiving, and the congratulatory note telling them when they will be starting. Seeing the intricate details of that letter, the individual letters and words offering them the job, the intricate details of their start date and more. I know that I keep repeating step 2 but it is really important to do your best to minimize or ignore distractions for these few minutes and to really focus on the visual.

Friends, the more you focus on the fine details and make them real, the closer you get to its manifestation. God rewards (as I said earlier) your efforts with this and He will always do His part to bring the good things to come to pass. What I am covering in this book is understanding the part that God plays and also understanding your part.

Feel It!

I cannot overstate the importance of feeling the really good feelings associated with the realized dream that you are trying to cause to manifest. For some people, I know this can be a challenge, so I invite you to take that challenge. Feel it as deeply as you can. I have heard of people grinning ear-to-ear when they are feeling that goodness, who shout out "Woohoo!", who cry tears of joy and more. All of these things are important feelings to allow yourself to feel because they allow you to get much closer to the manifestation.

A Replica

Something else that is tremendously effective in bringing about manifestation is to create (as closely as possible) a replica of the thing you are hoping to achieve and then putting it up so that you see it all the time. You can create a replica of the doctor's good report, a replica of the employment offer, a replica of the exact engagement ring and wedding band that you would like, a replica of the publishing contract you hope to get, a replica of the offer of admission with full scholarship that you are hoping for, a replica of the exact home you are looking to buy or build, a replica of the cheque you are hoping to receive, and more.

You can easily look up what a replica of that item might look like and do your best to make it as similar as possible. I suggest doing something as simple as taking a piece of paper and creating that replica with some simple markers or tools you have and as long as you are making it 1) as realistic as possible to you 2) putting in all the detail that you would like to see, then you are doing your part. Remember, this is your version of what the manifestation will look like. It does not mean that this is exactly what the real thing will look like but it's as close as we can get to it for the time being.

I remember before I got my first publishing contract many, many years ago, I had written a replica of my new job via email but forgetting to include the details of the kind of offer I was hoping to receive, the terms, etc. I was still new to manifesting so I didn't know to include all those details. Sure enough, the offer came that responded to all the items I had included and even though I was grateful to have received any publishing contract at all, it wasn't as I would have wanted because I had to learn this concept - add lots of detail. Please don't get me wrong, I was still very grateful for the contract - I just wished that I had included the additional information, allowing me to be more specific with my vision and therefore more likely to receive the exact manifestation I was hoping for.

What's also great about creating a replica is the fact that it causes us to think about all the details of relating to our ask and therefore, causes us to be more specific about what we are asking for in the manifestation. For example, for the person imagining their marriage certificate, there are different types of marriage ceremonies, and different places you can officially be married. Envisioning and creating your marriage certificate for visualization purposes will help you think about those pieces. Even the smallest detail such as how the font will be that includes your name and the name of your spouse is important and can make it more real to you.

I remember when I would envision getting engaged, I would do my best to feel the ridges of the ring on that finger, doing my best to see the velvet box that encases the ring and envisioning the way the marriage certificate would look.

A person can want a pet or a family. Having a picture of the kind of pet you would like (a puppy, a dog, a cat, a chicken, a turtle, etc.) will help to really narrow things down and help you be more specific. Saying "I want a family" is very general: do you want to get married and have a family, do you want to be a step-parent, do you want a set of friends that are so tight-knit that you are like a family? All good and important things to consider. Having a family is great - do you consider pets as part of your family, how many children, do you want the children to be biologically yours, do you want to adopt children, how many children, etc.?

Circle of Trust

I am reminded of this term from the movie Meet the Fockers. The bride's father (played by Robert DeNiro) invites his potential new son-in-law into what he called "the circle of trust". As its name suggests, this is a circle available to not only people who would be deemed worthy of that trust, but they have all in some ways proven that they are worthy of that trust.

My reason for mentioning this is that everyone needs to have people they trust in their circle. You do not need many, really, but having some would be helpful. Instead of asking you to jot down who you would put in your circle, I will instead invite you to pray about who God would have you put in your circle. Remember that He knows the hearts and the intentions of everyone, so He would be in the best position to know what you need and whom to add into this circle.

Here is a suggested prayer you can use to ask God about this and you can use the space provided to jot down the answers He provides or where you feel He is guiding you:

God, You know the hearts, minds and intentions of people. You know their every inner thought, feeling and motivation. As per Christine's book, I am looking to include select people into my circle of trust and I am asking You to bless me with Your wisdom and knowledge about whom to include in the circle. Please give me the names of the people You would like me to include in the circle and/or provide their faces into my mind so I know whom You are referring to, so that I may jot down the names and how you would like me to approach these select people for this task. I pray for Your great wisdom in this regard. In Jesus' name. Amen.

I'd like to give you a moment now to do that and to see what comes. You can use the space here to jot down what you feel you have gotten. Remember, you can always ask for more information and more details as you get names and see faces.

_____
_____
_____
_____
_____
_____
_____
_____
_____
_____
_____
_____

Praying the prayer above will help open the door to God providing you with the right people to include, so that you know that your circle of trust is populated and inhabited by the right people. It's an important matter so it's important to take the time to do this step correctly. There is also nothing wrong with writing out the names you feel you are getting, setting it aside for some time, and then coming back to revisit it and see that you feel you have gotten this right.

Today...Maybe Not Next Year

Now, I also want to point out something important here: **just because a person is included in your circle of trust today, it doesn't mean that they will always remain in your circle.** What do I mean by this? The old saying that a person can come into your life for a reason or a season is very true and perhaps, once their role in your life is complete, it may not mean that they will remain in the circle or in your life. I have watched many people come and go from my life and from the life of those around me and I have watched other people inspired to not include some people in their circle. It can definitely be unfortunate to lose someone because they are no longer meant to be in your life and it can be even harder to lose someone because they have passed away but it's most important to check-in with God regularly and to keep seeing that these same people are the ones who should be in your circle.

A lady I was ministering to hadn't updated her list in quite some time. She was continuing to seek out the same people from her circle of trust as before but was noticing that there were all of sudden, many more challenges in her way than before. I advised her to pray to see if all those people should remain in the circle. She did so and she immediately came back to me with the response "I was supposed to leave out this person long ago". The person in question had a change of heart toward the woman and was now actively trying to work against her. When she had said that she was praying for her, she was, in fact, praying against her. This is something that was brought to light by her prayers, as God revealed to her the change of heart this woman had. Things certainly continued to move forward positively after that!

I had the experience of watching someone I thought was a great guy (I will name him Vahe) fall completely from grace and be cut out of his best friend's life entirely because he was no chose to no longer follow God but had turned over to dark ways. This massive change was a huge shock to everyone who knew him and unfortunately, he could not be trusted anymore, so needless to say he had to be taken out of the circle of trust. It was a huge blow to the family and friends of this man but his turn in life was a fact and it had begun to be dangerous to include him in the circle.

I want to point out that when a person is on the wrong path, as friends, close ones and loved ones, we should be able to talk to them and help them see that their ways are wrong in an effort to bring them back but the choice remains there. In other words, it is their free choice to start or continue to follow the Lord or to turn their backs.

I also want to mention that I don't advise people to cut others from their circle flippantly. It can be a very hard thing to do and I don't make light of it. For most, peoples' circles are a very important and meaningful part of their lives and so much care and thought needs to go into making the decision to keep someone or to make changes.

Your Motivators, Encouragers

Those in your circle are meant to be your motivators, and the people who encourage you when things get tough. When your dreams have not yet manifested and you feel like the process may not be working or working fast enough, we need to rely on the goodness, kindness and motivation provided by our motivators to help us through the difficult times.

People who are in your circle of trust must and need to know that they are there. You really should not have a person in that circle who does not know they are there because they need to be advised that they are in a strong position of responsibility in your life. A conversation and an agreement (verbal is fine) that they are in your circle is advised so that they know they have the honor of being in that circle.

I also want to point out that just because a person is in your circle, as indicated and advised by God, it does not necessarily mean that you will also, in turn, be in theirs. This may be a difficult concept and realization for many to accept but it is fact. You can be in someone's circle but not necessarily be in theirs.

I recall when something similar to this happened to me and it was a bit of a pill for me to swallow. I discovered that the person was in my circle but that I was not in theirs and they respectfully explained to me why I was not in theirs: I was (at that time) a very new Christian and simply did not have the know-how, the knowledge base, or the experience that was needed to be in the circle. For this particular person, it is something I had to build up to and work toward by growing in my maturity with the Lord. Today, I am grateful to have the people in my circle that I do because they have each been hand selected for one reason or another.

One last word about people being in your circle of trust: a good friend of mine is in my circle and when I told her about a work situation some time ago and how my boss at the time was treating me, she told me that things didn't sound right at all with the way I was being treated. I was at a low point in my life and hadn't seen what my friend pointed out to me. I had to take some time with it and I realized how right she was in her interpretation of the events and how downright rude this boss had been to me. Today, I look back on this as a teachable moment to say that not every boss will be good to you or will see your value. I realized that I had to go to work with the Lord as my Boss, and not this woman. All this to say that people in your circle can provide some pretty great nuggets of help and wisdom to you that you can later pray over to see what the Holy Spirit is saying to you about it.

20

Seeing It When It Is Not Yet Physically There

Visualizing basically means seeing something that is not yet there. Biblically, we are presented with this Scripture: (Hebrews 11: "Now faith is being sure of what we hope for and certain of what we do not yet see"). It means that we are looking with the eyes of faith to see things as real before they appear in front of us. This is one of the core concepts and basis for visualization and manifestation. We are using the eyes of our hearts and the eyes of our imagination to see what does not yet exist in the physical in front of us.

I never considered myself to be good at art. In school, I feel I was a miserable failure at art and I don't remember my teachers ever telling me I had any artist prowess, ability or know-how. But the good news is that visualizing does not depend on your artistic vision or know-how; it depends on the vision God gives you and so we need to be able to pray to the Holy Spirit to give us the vision we need to focus our vision on.

> **We have to see things not as they are but as God sees them.**

When God told Abraham he would have descendants as many as the stars in the sky, meanwhile Abraham had not one child, Abraham must have been totally confused and perplexed by this. He and his wife were approaching 100 years in age and it was no longer biologically realistic for them to conceive; how, then, could God be saying to him that he would have a biological son and as many descendants as there are stars in the sky. Same thing for Mary, a virgin who would get pregnant and have a son? David, a poor shepherd boy becoming royalty? It seems inconceivable until God gets involved.

Visualizing works in the same way: God has told you it is going to happen, and that you have to do these things to access it, therefore it will. You may not see a way but that doesn't mean that He doesn't have a way. I have watched miracle after miracle happen in my life, in the life of family and friends and people all around me when they have chosen to have the faith to trust in God and His promises. When you visualize, and you pay attention to the visual, focusing on it, seeing in almost like in 3D and seeing the

Exercise: Let's take a moment right now to do an exercise and in this exercise, we are going to focus on the feelings of that vision. In other words, we are going to focus on what it feels like to actually be (right now) in possession of that thing. We are going to work on making this real to ourselves so that we are able to get a real sense of what possessing "that thing" means in our lives today.

Please take the following steps:

1. Get yourself to a quiet place and space where you will not

likely be interrupted for some time. It may be helpful to sit in a comfortable space and in a comfortable way to do this.

2. Close your eyes and get yourself to be totally still in a way that is comfortable but that also encourages you to stay alert (and not to fall asleep). Take a few minutes to really get to this relaxed state - there is no rush and being totally in this relaxed state will really help the process so make sure you take your time and do this step.
3. Pray this prayer in your mind: "*Lord, please give me visuals of blessings You want to bring to my life.*"
4. Wait and let this happen. It may not happen right away, it may take some time for part or all of the image to form in your mind. If it takes some time, that's ok. Don't rush this.
5. When you begin to see the image forming or it is fully formed, ask the Lord to show you and/or talk to you about the individual, intricate details of everything about it.
6. Pay attention to all parts of it and to the feelings that will inevitably come when you are seeing it. Whatever emotions you feel looking at it, go with it, especially if they are happy or positive ones.
7. Remain on this and with the feelings for several minutes.
8. If you are able, pray that the Lord shows you any actions or steps you need to take now or in the near future in this regard.

As you begin to visualize, you will begin to see things, circumstances, people, etc., move in your life. You will see shifts happening that, later on in hindsight, you will likely see as having been instrumental to the formation and to the manifestation of this visual. You don't need to understand how all the pieces are moving - just see that they are moving and that these things are the necessary route that need to be taken toward the fulfillment of the vision.

When you are finished with the 8 steps above, come out of your meditation slowly, being careful not to jolt yourself out but to come out leisurely. It may take you a moment to come to and to remember your surroundings. Take your time with this. No rush.

Write out the feelings you felt, the experience you had with this. This is meant to be a regular (hopefully daily) practice so it is a good idea to write out your feelings and your experience so that you can see later how you felt with this and you can track your feelings, progress and results. Microscopically tiny details help to "activate" the vision, we are giving life to it by our activation and our focus on it and we, as co-creators with God, are actually creating it with Him.

Challenges When Visualizing, Praying & Meditating

No matter who you are, and no matter how long you have been praying and visualizing and meditating, you will always face challenges. These can be smaller challenges or bigger ones, but regardless, you will face challenges. They can be challenges in terms of interruptions or disruptions when you are trying to pray, visualize or meditate, challenges in people trying to dissuade you from engaging in these practices, or people who try to get you to take your eyes off of Jesus. I can tell you that these challenges will come because I have faced many of them myself and it takes work, patience, perseverance and more to stay focused and stay the course.

The Challenge Is Designed to Help You

One of the truest statements I have heard is that we should not always just wish our challenges away. Our challenges were never meant to stop us. God would never have allowed the challenge to occur if it could stop us and His plan for us. Instead, we need to use the challenges to propel us, to show our true colors, to persevere through. I take the example of Judas. Judas' betrayal (the challenge) is the very thing Jesus needed to successfully complete His mission. Without Judas' betrayal, we don't know if Jesus would have fulfilled what He was called to fulfill.

He posed significant challenges to Jesus but his presence was meant to propel Jesus to fulfilling His purpose and achieving His glory, not to hinder it. Without this challenge, Jesus would not have been able to demonstrate His discipline, power and faith in God.

The same is true of the challenge you face today. God did not allow it to come if it was going to be powerful enough to stop you from fulfilling your purpose. Instead, use it as a means to fuel your faith, fuel your motivation and fuel your sense of co-creating with God to bring about His goodness despite the challenges that lay ahead of you.

Carol is an indie author, working on her first books. She was new to the industry so it was taking her some time to really understand the givens of what she was working with and how to properly navigate the literary landscape. As she was trying to promote her book, one bookseller told her that he was refusing to carry her books because "there was no interest in them." Carol was crushed. She took the news very badly and she took it as a major shot against her self-esteem, her writing abilities and more. I told her the same thing I am telling you: God wouldn't have allowed the challenge if it was powerful enough to stop you. Keep pressing ahead, keep praying, keep visualizing and keep meditating. You and God are a majority.

Another example that comes to mind is that of Joe. Joe was desperate to get his landscaping business up-and-running. He was trying very hard to make all the right connections, do all the right things, etc. Because his was a new business, he didn't have much money for advertising and for promotions. He was relying on word of mouth. Out of nowhere (and still in the midst of his struggle), Joe faced a new competitor in town who was offering the same service as him. He thought "I wasn't even making money before this new competitor came in. Now I'll never make a dime." He began to pray, to visualize and to meditate on the promises he felt God made to him, that He would bless his business. Slowly, Joe started to get a slow trickle of customers, one at first, then two, three and then ten. Things were starting up but he was nowhere near where he needed to be still. He kept on praying, meditating and visualizing in faith. Two months later, Joe received word from a customer that his competitor was cutting corners, using substandard supplies, and being dishonest about his labor and costs. People were starting to get the impression that his competitor was a dishonest businessman, out to hurt (not help) his customers. Joe kept working in an honest manner, in good faith and continued to pray that God would bless his business. A large scandal broke out and Joe's competitor went out of business, and faced a class action lawsuit for his dishonest business dealings, meanwhile Joel was getting ahead as an honest and trustworthy landscaper. See how Joe's faith, prayers, meditation and visualizing of the success God promised him propelled him to much greater success. Without that challenging competitor, people would not have been as keenly aware and appreciative of Joe's good and honest service, propelling him to success.

FAQ Section

Here are some frequently asked questions about manifesting. Hopefully these will help answer any lingering questions, thoughts or worries you may have.

Q: Can there be too many items on my vision board?
A: Nope. It's your vision board so you are welcome and encouraged to include as many things as you'd like. Put things that are meaningful to you and that you will know what you mean when you see the image. In an effort to keep Jesus top-of-mind, put His name or a cross somewhere on your board, given that it is He that will be blessing you.

Q: What if I'm not sure so I want to put 2-3 variations of one thing?
A: Of course. It has to make sense to you.

Q: Can I include words on my vision board?
A: Yes. That is a good idea. Words and even phrases are great and helpful.

Q: If I stop visualizing after having visualized for a long time, will that thing still manifest?

A: Not very likely. The practice requires sustained faith and sustained focus. When you stop, the progress halts.

Q: I complained. Will that mean I won't get what I asked for?
A: The best thing to do is to repent for complaining and then continue to pray, visualize and meditate. Complaining is a big way to stop the blessing.

Q: Can I visualize success for someone else?
A: Yes, you can but you may want to ensure you have had a conversation with them about this and that they know you are doing this for them. Visualization is a deeply personal practice and the person needs to be on-board. You cannot force someone to do this nor should you.

Q: What is the minimum amount of time per day that I should visualize in order to make something manifest?
A: A minimum of 15 minutes every day.

Q: What do I do if I keep getting distracted?
A: It is perfectly normal for that to happen. I suggest you turn off your phone or put your phone on do not disturb (DND), get to a private room, tell people you need 20 minutes so please don't bother you during that time, and pray for God to eliminate distractions are just some things you can do to help eliminate distractions. Remember, this is your time and your practice so you have to make it a priority.

Q: What if I have some doubt? Will it still work?
A: It will work as long as you have faith as small as a mustard seed but do your best to believe in God's promises and pray for God to increase your faith in this.

Q: Am I allowed to pray for and visualize receiving money? Is that bad? A: There is nothing wrong with calling forth money. The

Lord calls us to work hard, to make money and to use your financial resources wisely, and to be good stewards of the financial abundance He has given you.

Q: Can I ask God to shorten the waiting time? Is that valid?

A: Of course, you can ask for that. Remember that prayer, praise, worship and thanksgiving to God also go a long way and help the manifestation come more quickly.

Q: Can I ask others to visualize and pray for me, to help with my own efforts?

A: Absolutely. God sees and rewards all your efforts, even when you ask others to support you by praying for you. Many Churches and organizations have shared weekly prayer lists that you may want to consider participating in.

Q: I have not done what I feel I was guided to do. Will this still work?

A: You must do as He guides, in the way He guides and in the measure with which He guides. Faith without works is dead.

Q: I feel He is taking someone out of my circle of trust. How can I be sure before I take action on it?

A: Pray for Him to provide clarity and wisdom on the matter. Also ask for how He would have you approach this if it is, in fact, guiding you to not include that person any longer. Also, check-in with your safety checkers to see what they have to say about that.

Q: Part of what I asked for manifested, but not all. What should I do?

A: Keep visualizing, praying and working strategically. You can see it is working so why stop? Focus your eyes now on the part that hasn't manifested yet and remember to thank the Lord for what has manifested so far.

Q: I am doing what I need to do but it seems all the doors are closing in my face. Now what?

A: God can open any doors closed by man, if they are the right doors. Ask Him what He would have you do and to open (or create) new doors that you will need.

Q: I don't feel I have a great imagination. How do I do this visualization thing?

A: Start small and ask the Holy Spirit for help in expanding or enhancing your current vision. Remember, the vision ultimately comes from God, not from you, so pray and ask for all the details you will need to be able to see about this. Ask Him to bring you a clear vision and to show you all parts of it.

21

The Courage To Manifest

Manifesting takes courage.

It takes courage to spend the time every day seeing, visualizing, and taking the strategic actions that are necessary to produce the results that we are looking for. God has put a dream on your heart or he has put many dreams on your heart and those dreams take work, patience, perseverance and prayer. There are no free lunches here. We need to make sure that we are using the tools we have been given to visualize based on what God is showing us and has promised us, and we need to make sure that we are taking the strategic actions necessary to do these things in the time frame He provides.

Some people might say "Christine, who am I to visualize?" or "Why should I spend my time doing this?" The simple and honest answer to that is that you have greatness within you that God has put there for a reason, and God has given you a destiny that is just yours. He has given us (every single one of us) the tools to accomplish everything that we need to. Those tools can include your specific personality, your sense of humor, your height, the way you think, and so much more. You have been uniquely, wonderfully, and fearfully well-made. If God has not opened a certain door for you, it's because you don't need that door to be opened. You may be tempted to look at somebody else and to say " Why do you think God put this particular quality in me?" The simple answer is that you are going to need that quality to do what He has called you to do. Let me explain this point further: God has given you everything that you require in order to accomplish your purposes and to reach your dreams. He has not given you what you will need to reach the dreams of somebody else. To that person, he has given them everything that they need. A wonderful indicator, therefore, that tells you where your purposes and your calling lie and what you are meant to do in your life are going to be governed by the gifts that he has put inside of you. So this is the point in the book at which I will remind you that in order to fulfill your specific purpose, you will need those specific gifts.

To one person, He may have given the gift of being an artist and having great vision for artistic pieces. To another, He has put in them the gift of being an amazing brain surgeon so that you can save people's lives. To another, He has given the gift of being able to teach, while to another has been given the gift of creating beautiful clothes and envisioning wonderful fashion outfits. There are so many amazing gifts and things that we can do with each of the amazing gifts He has provided and so we need to be sure and confident to use our gifts in the best ways He instructs.

A few years ago, I remember watching somebody at work who was doing amazing things and receiving many accolades for that work. I watched them carefully and I watched to see how they were doing what they were doing and the ease with which they were doing it. It didn't feel great to my ego because simply put, I wanted to be able to do those wonderful things too. But their path was not my path. My path is a wonderful one that is different from that of other people's and it would be foolish of me to spend time, energy, and effort on working fruitlessly toward someone else's path and misusing my energy and talents. Instead, if I am looking at my own path, I need to realize that I have certain gifts and certain qualities that make me uniquely qualified to do the things that God has put on my heart!

Any goal and any dream is going to require your dedication and your focus. How can you remain focused and dedicated to your goals if you are looking to someone else to see what is on their path as opposed to paying attention to what is on yours?

Greatness Is In You

Every single person has greatness within them. Every single person has wonderful traits and qualities that are innate to them. Nobody else can have the qualities that you have and do the things that you do in the exact same way that you do them. I'm going to use the example of some contractors that I needed to use for some work that I needed done in my home. While the contractors technically did do the same work, the way that they approached it, the way they spoke to me, the intricacies of their work, and the way that they explained everything that needed to be done to me was completely different one from the other. My point is that not everyone is called to do this work and when you see that you take great joy and do your work with love and with glee, you know you are using your gifts for the right purpose.

Take a few moments right now and ask yourself where your particular skill sets lie. What have you been told that you are really good at and that you know in your heart that you do differently than everybody else. Like with David in Scripture, we may think that our skill (in David's case it was being great with a slingshot) is not anything significant or anything to really consider significant. But that thinking is wrong. Your particular skill or skills is and are vitally important for the destiny that you have. For the particular destiny that is in front of you, that is the exact skill that you need in order to accomplish your purposes. David's skill with a slingshot is what ended up catapulting him to the Kingdom, by defeating Goliath. There was not anybody else around who could have defeated the giant in that simple and quick of a way. What David was able to do with that simple skill (simple but important) is that he was able to fulfill his purpose.

A woman that I knew was wonderful at playing piano and she enjoyed playing her piano every day for hours on end. You could see the joy of life in her face as she played that piano and as she got to perform pieces in different ways, with different styles, and with an effortless ease that was amazing. Some might say that she just has the skill of playing the piano. What's so great about that? What's so great about that is that she has one wonderful skill that ended up catapulting her to a different level. Even though she was a wonderful piano player, she ended up having an accident in her early teens which left her unable to play. Initially, she was completely distraught because playing piano was so meaningful to her and she loved it so much. It was a part of her life. A wise friend then advised her that she should continue piano playing but it didn't necessarily mean that she had to be the one playing. What her friend was basically advising her to do was to teach piano. She had never really considered that as an option before because playing gave her the greatest joy but she decided to consider it to see if maybe teaching piano would be something that she would like to do and that she felt led to do by the Holy Spirit. Sure enough, she ended up reporting that playing the piano gave her great joy but that teaching piano was absolutely even more joyful to her because it allowed her not only to hear the music but it allowed her to pass on her skill to next generations. Through teaching, she was able to pass on her skills and knowledge of playing the piano to many different children, teens and adults and was able to spread her joy to many more people than she ever was able to when she was playing just for herself and by herself.

I want to make a point here that even though we may think that our skill set is not important or we only look at it as serving our lives in one way, there are amazing things that we can do with even one skill that we have and we never know how that is going to end up touching lives of all the people around us. We need to be open to seeing the use and practice of our skills from more than one angle. This lady also revealed to me that on her vision board, she included pictures of some of the greatest piano teachers in the world and how they taught their students to be incredible players. She hadn't intended it as a gateway to becoming a piano teacher but it ended up bringing this subconsciously into her life by the use of a vision board and manifestation.

Manifesting Can Take Some Time

Manifesting can take time but be of the comforting knowledge that when we begin visualization to manifest, things begin to move immediately into favor for us to manifest our desire(s). In other words, as soon as we begin to visualize or as soon as God has given us that dream and a vision, the process of manifestation has begun.

Visualizing and manifesting are also wonderful ways of affirming that we understand the tools that God has given us and that we are accepting them and their application in order to bring God's best into our lives. Some people might be of the thought that *"this is going to take too long to manifest"* or *"I'm not special enough to manifest anything."* These are lies. Every single one of us is very special and God has put the ability to do this in every single one of us. He has given us the ability to co-create with Him in an effort to show us that not only are we supposed to depend on Him but for the manifestation of our dreams and goals but that we are also supposed to do our part as best as we can. We have to be able to take action and do the things that we need to do. God helps those who help themselves and who follow His guidance and strategic actions to accomplish the purposes He has put on your heart. He can put all the dreams He wants on your heart but if you don't take the time to actually listen, obey and perform the strategic actions, you are not going to get anywhere near the fulfillment of the promise. You not getting anywhere does not mean that God didn't do his part. It means that you did not do yours.

"Christine, I don't have time to do this consistently"

Visualizing is not generally something you do one time and then consider your role to be complete. It is something that needs to be done again and again, in order to continue moving things in the right direction. Some people say that they don't have time to dedicate to this. While I understand respectfully that everybody has many things to do, not taking the time to visualize means that you are not putting in the time or the effort that is required to accomplish and manifest what you say is very important to you.

When we speak about our dreams and our goals, we are speaking about things that are very important to us. Don't those things require your time, care, dedication and attention? When I was looking to cause my very first chapter book to manifest (something I found very difficult to do), I was presented with a vision for how the Lord wanted my book to look. He downloaded the image, the words, and the messages of the book as well as the feel and tone of that first book entitled Jesus Loves You, into me. I could have ignored the vision. I could have refused to write down the words. I could have said that I was too busy with other things, and a myriad of other excuses. But I didn't. What I did do was grab a piece of paper that was nearby and I began to furiously write down the words that I was getting. Truth be told, I never set out to be a writer or an author. It is a dream that I had in my heart but it is not something I ever saw coming to fruition. That day, the vision that I got from the Lord changed that because I realized that He was the one who gave me the desire to do this and as such, He was going to bring me all I needed in order to accomplish it.

I have since used prayer, visualization and much meditation to accomplish the literary goals He has given me and I dedicated myself to also writing chapter books.

Writing books of all kinds has taken so much more time, energy and effort than I ever thought it would. Not only do you have to conceptualize the book, you need to write down the words, the images that are going to accompany, you need to ensure the formatting is correct, you need to select the right publisher if you are going to use a publisher, you need to make sure that the spelling of the grammar are correct, you need to market in promote your book in order for the world to know about it. When it comes to chapter books, we are talking about a completely different ballgame because that, in my experience and opinion, requires more time and attention.

What am I saying?

When we are working towards a dream and a goal, we have to dedicate ourselves and realize that it is going to take time and effort. If we choose to give up midway, that is our choice as people with free will but understand that it will mean that you have not accomplished the purposes that you were called to do. I therefore encourage you to get up and pray and do the things that you are being led to do, which are going to lead to the manifestation of your dreams. Ask God to help you every step of the way to make sure that you are doing what needs to be done and that you are being held accountable for what you are able to do. In Scripture, David didn't just walk away from the situation and say "I can't defeat Goliath and I'm not even going to bother trying. It takes too much time and effort. " He went ahead and he had faith that he would defeat that giant, and he did.

The Challenges Will Come

I have said this before but it bears repeating. In life, we are going to have challenges. That is inevitable and Jesus told us we would have challenges in this world. Whether you are at the starting point of working towards your goals or you are at the midpoint or at any point really, you are going to experience them. What is going to set you apart and what is going to cause you to accomplish those goals is how you handle the challenges.

Are you going to allow that difficulty to be what stops you?
Are you going to allow those challenges to overtake you and make you stop reaching and striving for your goals?
Are you going to allow people who are unsupportive and downright mean stop you from working and achieving?

These are the important questions you need to ask yourself. When my sister-in-law was pregnant with hers and my brother's first, the doctor told her that she was going to be experiencing a very difficult pregnancy. I watched how for months, she went through challenge after challenge, was described as a "special case", and had to make numerous trips to the hospital in order to make sure the baby was healthy. She would sometimes call me from the hospital and she would be in tears, worried about the health of the baby and wondering why this was happening. I'm telling you the same thing that I told her: stick with it, this too shall pass, and we need to do everything that we can think of that is going to move things forward in the right ways, along with praying. When the baby was finally delivered happy and healthy on January 26, she got to see the manifestation of their dream of being parents of a happy and healthy baby. She got to see how overcoming the challenges that came end up causing her to be a stronger person in the end and to know how to deal with future challenges when they do come. You have that same greatness within you.

Wrong or Bad Past Moves

As humans, we make mistakes. We've all been there and done that.

Some moves are not so permanent in their lasting effects, while others are.

When you work with God to co-create, He will bring to light the mistakes and errors in a loving way and will give you a chance to fix them. He will always give a new opportunity to fix, repair and make better the areas where you have gone wrong and that may be blocking you or preventing you from achieving all that He has called you to achieve.

Some people reading this may think *"Christine, you don't know how badly I have messed things up. You don't have a clue about the pain I have caused, the errors I have made and the missteps I have made."* I don't know but God does. And He still loves you and still says you can come to Him for love, for help and to turn things around. He will always love you & support you by meeting you where you are and so yes, the gifts of the tools of prayer, meditation and visualization are for you too.

Happy Manifesting!

22

Thoughts and Reflections

I'd like to give you this space to really think & reflect about manifesting. Now that you have read through the book (hopefully) and have learned a bit (more...again, hopefully), I'd like to give you an opportunity to think & meditate on all you have learned and how you would like to move forward with this, in an effort to improve your life and the lives of those around you.

I encourage you to keep this reflection in a safe space so that you can revisit it later, and add to it over the coming hours, days, weeks, months and years. This is your space to reflect & to grow.

Please also remember that we have a prayer & support community at my site, DrChristineTopjian.com and you are always welcome to create an account and to join, partake and benefit from the community. It was created with you, dear reader, in mind.

_____
_____
_____
_____

MANIFEST IT!

MANIFEST IT! — 171

MANIFEST IT! ~ 173

About the Author

Dr. Christine Topjian is an Award-winning author, and writer. She wears many hats and enjoys helping people understand and reach their best lives in Christ through coaching, sermons, books, presentations and more.

She lives in Toronto, Ontario with her family.

Feel free to check out the many other books by Dr. Topjian available online and in bookstores.

www.ingramcontent.com/pod-product-compliance
Lightning Source LLC
Chambersburg PA
CBHW051705160426
43209CB00004B/1028